Proceedings of the

FOURTH BIENNIAL INTERNATIONAL

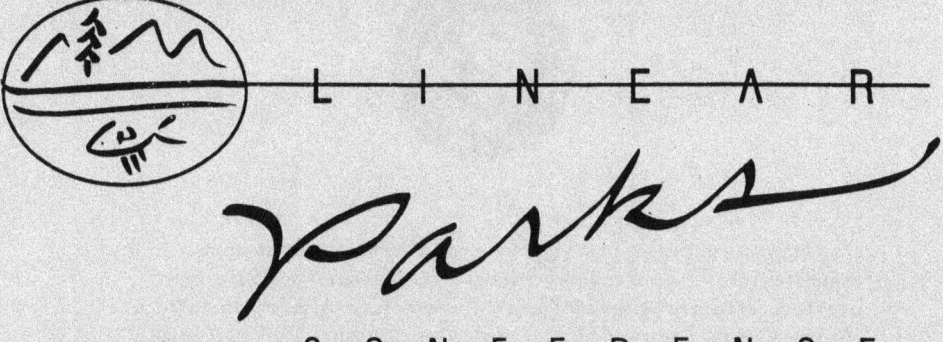

LINEAR Parks

CONFERENCE

November 12-14, 1991
Charlottesville, Virginia

*Parkways, Greenways, Riverways:
A Partnership for Beauty and Progress*

Appalachian Consortium Press
Boone, North Carolina 28608

The Appalachian Consortium was a non-profit educational organization composed of institutions and agencies located in Southern Appalachia. From 1973 to 2004, its members published pioneering works in Appalachian studies documenting the history and cultural heritage of the region. The Appalachian Consortium Press was the first publisher devoted solely to the region and many of the works it published remain seminal in the field to this day.

With funding from the Andrew W. Mellon Foundation and the National Endowment for the Humanities through the Humanities Open Book Program, Appalachian State University has published new paperback and open access digital editions of works from the Appalachian Consortium Press.

www.collections.library.appstate.edu/appconsortiumbooks

This work is licensed under a Creative Commons BY-NC-ND license. To view a copy of the license, visit http://creativecommons.org/licenses.

Original copyright © 1991 by the Appalachian Consortium Press.

ISBN (pbk.: alk. Paper): 978-1-4696-4214-7
ISBN (ebook): 978-1-4696-4217-8

Distributed by the University of North Carolina Press
www.uncpress.org

**1991 Fourth Biennial International
Linear Parks Conference**

*Parkways, Greenways, Riverways:
A Partnership for Beauty and Progress*

Contents

The Virginia Congressional Delegation and the Blue Ridge Parkway
Philip A. Grant, Jr. 4

America's Unprotected Scenic Corridors: The Quest for a National Policy
Helen Cozzetto and Don Cozzetto 10

Historic Resorts: Rediscovery of an American Legacy
Judy Byrd Brittenum 22

The Appalachian Trail Across the Cumberland Valley
Neil P. Korostoff, Thomas G. Yahner, Timothy P. Johnson 33

A Visual Assessment of the New River
Wayne E. Williams, Delmar W. Barchert,
Paul L. Gaskill, and Holly Pierce 46

Roanoke River Corridor Study, Phases I and II
Helen Smythers 52

An Interactive Recreation Demand/Supply Model for Personal Computers
Herman F. Senter and James P. Jarvis 56

The Use of Computer Animation in Developing Interpretive
Facilities Along the San Juan Skyway
James L. Sipes and Richard F. Ostergaard 68

Metro Green: A Greenway Proposal for Kansas City
Stephanie A. Rolley 74

Visual and Environmental Concerns for the Higashi Fujigoko Highway in Japan
Shigeo Sudo 84

Concept Plan for the Highlands Scenic Tour
Micheal L. O'Brien, William E. Shepherd, and Sarah Duncan 91

Three Pennsylvania Linear Parks 92
    The National Road: A Traveller's Landscape
        Stephanie Sechrist 93
    Heritage Park and Historic Riverway in the Pennsylvania Oil Region
        Randy Mason 97
    The Delaware & Lehigh Canal: Heritage Development in
    Perspective—Whole Places and New Partners in Linear Parks
        T. Allan Comp 102

Development of a State Roadside Vegetation Management Plan in Wisconsin
    Paul E. Skidmore and Bruce F. Woods 109

Selection of Alternative Routes for the Southern Extension of the New River Parkway
    Sarah Duncan and William E. Shepherd 118

Concept Plan for the New River Parkway
    William E. Shepherd and Sarah Duncan 122

The Southern Appalachian Man and the Biosphere Cooperative
    Hubert Hinote 139

The Virginia Congressional Delegation and the Blue Ridge Parkway

Philip A. Grant, Jr.

On March 4, 1933, Franklin D. Roosevelt was sworn in as the thirty-second president of the United States. Five days later, the newly inaugurated chief executive summoned the Seventy-Third Congress into emergency session. Between the opening ceremonies on March 9, 1933, and the formal adjournment of the Seventy-Fourth Congress on June 20, 1936, the House of Representatives and United States Senate were to enact a substantial number and wide variety of significant laws. Many of the measures were designed to alleviate the acute sufferings caused by the Great Depression.

The foremost priorities of the first Roosevelt administration included combatting unemployment and improving highway transportation. Congress eagerly cooperated with the president in these areas and approved an impressive array of landmark bills to effect relief and recovery. One of the most noteworthy developments of the years between 1933 and 1936 was the establishment of the Blue Ridge Parkway.

Among the individuals vested with the responsibility of approving or rejecting Roosevelt's historic initiatives were the two U.S. senators and nine members of the House from Virginia. These gentlemen, like their colleagues from other parts of the nation, would cast votes on an exceptionally large number of bills and resolutions. Several of these congressional measures directly or indirectly involved the Blue Ridge Parkway.

In the Seventy-Third Congress, Virginia's two senators were Harry F. Byrd of Berryville and Carter Glass of Lynchburg. Among Virginia's members of the House were Representatives A. Willis Robertson of Lexington, Clifton A. Woodrum of Roanoke, and Thomas G. Burch of Martinsville. Byrd, Glass, Robertson, Woodrum, and Burch, each of whom would occupy chairmanships of major committees or subcommittees in their respective bodies, would offer strong support for the Blue Ridge Parkway during the New Deal period.[1]

The origins of the Blue Ridge Parkway could be traced to the National Industrial Recovery Act. Signed (NIRA) into law by President Roosevelt at the White House on June 16, 1933, the NIRA provided for a $3.3 billion federal public works program. One of the provisions of the statute was Section 205(a), which reads:

> Not less than $50 million of the amount made available by this act shall be allotted for (a) national forest highways, (b) national forest roads, trails, bridges, and related projects, (c) national park roads and trails in national parks approved or authorized.

The Virginia delegation in Congress favored the NIRA by a 9-1 majority.[2]

On December 5, 1933, the Public Works Administration (PWA), which had been established under the NIRA, decided that $4 million would be set aside for the construction of a scenic highway between the Shenandoah and Great Smoky Mountains National Parks. Two weeks later the decision of the PWA was transmitted to the director of the National Parks Service, thereby according official sanction to the planning of the future parkway.[3]

On February 5, 1934, a delegation of distinguished Virginians testified before a federal hearing presided over by representatives of the PWA, the National Park Service, and the Bureau of Public Roads. While there was a consensus that the parkway should proceed from the Shenandoah National Park to the Peaks of Otter in Bedford County, there were differences as to the precise direction of the remaining portion of the parkway southward to the North Carolina state line. Congressman John W. Flannagan, Jr., of Bristol favored a route that would run west of Roanoke through Botetort, Craig, Giles, Pulaski, Bland, Wythe, and Smyth Counties. By contrast, Flannagan's colleague, Congressman Burch, urged a route passing east of Roanoke through Franklin, Floyd, Carroll, Patrick, and Grayson Counties. It was finally decided that Burch's proposal would be adopted, thus guaranteeing that Virginia's two hundred and seventeen miles of the parkway would be located within the confines of the congressional districts represented by Robertson, Woodrum, and Burch.[4]

The second piece of legislation affecting the development of the Blue Ridge Parkway was the Federal Highway Act of 1934. The law went into operation on June 18, 1934, immediately after President Roosevelt affixed his signature. Section 2 of the act was worded:

> To further increase employment by providing for emergency construction of public highways and other related projects, there is hereby also authorized to be appropriated, out of any money in the Treasury, not otherwise appropriated, the sum of $24 million . . . to be expended for the survey, construction, reconstruction, and maintenance of highways, roads, trails, bridges, and related projects in national parks and monuments, national forests . . .

Although few Republicans had voiced objections to certain features of the Federal Highway Bill, it had a virtual certainty that the measure would pass the heavily Democratic House. A Republican motion to recommit the bill was rejected on a 257-85 roll call, and minutes later the bill was approved 255-26. Consistent with their stand on the NIRA of the previous year, Virginians in the House were aligned 9-0 against recommittal and 8-0 in favor of final passage.[5]

Augmenting the NIRA and the Federal Highway Act of 1934, the Federal Highway Act of 1936 authorized additional money for the Blue Ridge Parkway. Section 5 of the act stipulated:

> For the construction and maintenance of parkways, to give access to national parks and national monuments, or to become connecting sections of a national parkway plan, over lands to which title has been transferred to the United States by the States of by private individuals, there is hereby authorized to be appropriated the sum of $10 million for the fiscal year ending June 30, 1938, and $10 million for the fiscal year ending June 30, 1939; provided, that the location of such parkways upon public lands, national forests, or other federal reservations shall be determined by agreement between the department having jurisdiction over such lands and the National Park Service.

The Federal Highway Act of 1936 was not subjected to a serious challenge until the conference report was submitted to the entire House. Notwithstanding the criticisms leveled by certain Republicans, the conference report was adopted on a 238-87 tabulation. Eight Virginians in the House cast affirmative votes on the conference report, while the ninth member was absent for the official roll call.[6]

On April 24, 1936, Congressman Robert L. Doughton of North Carolina, whose district bordered on the southwestern corner of Virginia, introduced a bill provided for the administration and maintenance of the Blue Ridge Parkway by the Department of the Interior. On the following day, the Doughton Bill was favorably reported by the Committee on Public Lands. Only one paragraph in length, the Doughton Bill proposed that

> all lands and easements conveyed or to be conveyed by the States of Virginia and North Carolina for the right-of-way for the proposed parkway between the Shenandoah and Great Smoky Mountains National Parks, together with sites acquired or to be acquired for recreation areas in connection therewith, and a right-of-way of said parkway of a width sufficient to include the highway and all bridges, ditches, cuts, and falls appurtenant thereto, but not exceeding a maximum of two hundred feet through government-owned lands as designated on maps, heretofore or hereafter approved by the Secretary of the Interior, shall be known as the Blue Ridge Parkway and shall be administered and maintained by the Secretary of the Interior through the National Park Service.[7]

Securing recognition in the House chamber on June 20, 1936, Doughton offered a motion to suspend the rules and pass the bill to place the Blue Ridge Parkway under the jurisdiction of the Department of the Interior. Because of firm opposition from many Republicans, it seemed doubtful whether the Doughton Bill would attract the two-thirds majority required by House rules. Congressman Robertson of Virginia, stressing that the bill carried "no appropriation or authorization for appropriation," declared that the measure simply provided for the administration of the parkway "when built by an appropriate agency of the Department of the Interior." After hearing Robertson's explanation, the House voted 175-125 to suspend the rules. Unfortunately, this majority was twenty-five votes short of the necessary two-thirds ratio. Virginians in the House favored suspending the rules by a 6-0 margin.[8]

After experiencing the frustration of having his bill rejected, Doughton persuaded the Committee on Rules to recommend that the bill be approved by the House. According to House procedures, a resolution emanating from the Rules Committee needed only a simple majority for acceptance. Within minutes after the opening of floor debate, the House passed the Doughton Bill by a 145-131 majority. Voting 6-0 in favor of the Doughton Bill, the Virginia delegation provided nearly half of the fourteen vote margin of victory.[9]

Two weeks after the passage of the Doughton Bill, President Roosevelt dedicated the Shenandoah National Park. In an address at Big Meadows on July 3, 1936, the president thanked the men "who have opened the Shenandoah National Park and other parks for the use and enjoyment of our citizens." Emphasizing that the nation was "going to need many other young men as they come to manhood, need them for work like this—for other Shenandoahs," Roosevelt asserted:

> Is it a dream? Shall I perhaps be accused of an exaggerated passion for planning if I paint you a picture? You who are here know of the great usefulness to humanity which this Skyline Drive achieves from now on, of the greater usefulness which its extension, south through Virginia and North Carolina and Tennessee to the Great Smoky Mountains National Park will achieve.
>
> In almost every other part of the country there is a similar need for recreational areas, for parkways which will give to men and women of moderate means the opportunity, the invigoration and the luxury of touring and camping amid scenes of great natural beauty like this.[10]

During the Second Administration of Franklin D. Roosevelt the progress of the Blue Ridge Parkway was expedited by the annual bills funding the operations of the Department of the Interior.[11] would be the responsibility of two Virginians, Chairman Glass of the Senate Committee on Appropriations and Representative Woodrum, a senior member of the House Committee on Appropriations, to work with their committee colleagues in determining how much money would be designated for the National Park Service. Altogether the Department of the Interior Appropriation Acts of 1937, 1938, 1939, and 1940, provided that $17.5 million would be reserved exclusively for the Blue Ridge and Natchez Trace Parkways.[11]

Agreeing on appropriations for the Blue Ridge Parkway provoked minor controversy in 1937 and 1939. In 1937, the House rejected a Republican attempt to delete funding for the parkway on a standing vote of 123-21, while two years later an identical G.O.P. measure was defeated on a 113-7 standing vote.[12]

In 1937, Congressman Woodrum, denouncing the Republicans for opposing appropriations to build the Blue Ridge Parkway, argued that the parkway had been "authorized by an act of Congress, which was fundamental legislation, and upon this basis the States of Virginia and North Carolina have acted in good faith." Woodrum's Virginian colleague, Robertson, vigorously supporting Doughton's amendment to increase the 1937 appropriation for the Blue Ridge and Natchez Trace Parkways from $3 million to $5 million, contended that it should be "a source of great pride that we are the first and only nation in the world to construct along the top of a great mountain range a tourist drive that combines safety with great scenic value." The Doughton Amendment, favored by all nine Virginians in the House, was adopted on a 221-160 roll call.[13]

In 1939, Congressman Robertson complained that the vast majority of House Republicans were hostile to the Blue Ridge Parkway. Robertson was consoled, however, that the Republicans in his congressional district were "deeply and vitally interested in the construction of the Blue Ridge Parkway, destined to be the greatest scenic highway in the world."[14]

Throughout the New Deal era, Virginia ranked among the most solidly Democratic states in the nation. In 1936 and 1940, President Roosevelt carried Virginia by respective proportions of 70.5% and 68.4%. The chief executive fared especially well in several communities located in close proximity to the Blue Ridge Parkway, handily prevailing over his 1936 and 1940 Republican challengers in such cities as Roanoke, Staunton, and Buena Vista. Indeed, in 1936 and 1940, Roosevelt won the three Virginia congressional districts through which the Blue Ridge Parkway was being constructed by rather convincing margins. The levels of support for the president in these districts were:

	1936	1940
Fifth District	67.3%	70.1%
Sixth District	65.1%	66.4%
Seventh District	62.4%	60.5%

Inasmuch as a popular Democratic president strongly favored both the conservation of natural resources and highway construction, it should not have been particularly surprising that he was sympathetic to the Blue Ridge Parkway. The reality that the electorate of Virginia was so steadfastly loyal to Roosevelt was a factor which could not be ignored in terms of measures to facilitate the development of the parkway.[15]

Between 1933 and 1940, while both the House and Senate were firmly controlled by the Democratic party, all eleven Virginia congressmen were Democrats. Nine of the eleven members of the Virginia delegation served continuously throughout the first two Roosevelt administrations, and by 1940 these nine gentlemen had accumulated an aggregate total of one hundred and forty-four years of longevity on Capitol Hill. Serving on the Senate Committees on Appropriations and Finance and the House Committees on Appropriations, Ways and Means, and Post Offices and Post Roads, these congressmen, affiliated with the majority political party, were obviously in positions to wield influence over legislation affecting the Blue Ridge Parkway. The fact that the Blue Ridge Parkway was being constructed through three districts represented by congressmen from Virginia certainly had a bearing on the way members of the Virginia delegation viewed the entire question.[16]

NOTES

1. Raymond H. Pulley, "Carter Glass," *Dictionary of American Biography, Supplement Four* (New York: Charles Scribner's Sons, 1974), 330-332.

   Steve Neal, "Harry Flood Byrd," *Dictionary of American Biography, Supplement Eight* (New York: Charles Scribner's Sons, 1988), 67-69.

   Henry C. Ferrell, Jr., "Harry Flood Byrd," *Encyclopedia of Southern History* (Baton Rouge: Louisiana State University Press, 1979), 165-166.

   James E. Sargeant, "Clifton A. Woodrum of Virginia: A Southern Progressive in Congress, 1923-1945," *Virginia Magazine of History and Biography* 89 (July 1981): 341-364.

   Philip A. Grant, Jr., "Virginia's Congressional Committee Chairmen, 1911-1960." *Virginia Social Science Journal* 10 (April 1975): 51-55.

2. U.S. Congress, *Congressional Record* 77 (Washington, D.C.: GPO, 1933), 4062, 5692.

   The Statutes at Large of the United States of America, 1933-1935 48 (Washington, D.C., 1935), 195-211.

   Frank Freidel, *Franklin D. Roosevelt: Launching the New Deal* (Boston: Little, Brown and Company, 1973), 444-452.

   New York Times, 27 May 1933, 1.

   New York Times, 14 June 1933, 1.

3. Harley E. Jolley, *The Blue Ridge Parkway* (Knoxville: Univ. of Tennessee Press, 1969), 43-44.

   U.S. Department of the Interior, *Annual Report of the Secretary of the Interior, 1934*, (Washington, D.C.: GPO, 1934), 196.

4. T. H. Watkins, *Righteous Pilgrim: The Life and Times of Harold L. Ickes* (New York: Henry Holt and Company, 1990), 461-472.

   Jolley, 61, 86-87.

   U.S. Department of the Interior, *Annual Report of the Secretary of the Interior, 1935* (Washington, D.C.: GPO, 1935), 210.

5. U.S. Congress, *Congressional Record* 78 (Washington, D.C.: GPO, 1934), 8651-8652.

   Statutes at Large 48, 993-996.

   Frederick L. Paxson, "The Highway Movement, 1916-1935," *American Historical Review* 51 (January 1946), 236-253.

   New York Times, 19 July 1934, 1-2.

6. U.S. Congress, *Congressional Record* 80 (Washington, D.C.: GPO, 1936), 8704-8705.

   Statutes at Large 49, 1519-1522.

7. U.S. House, *Report No. 2544*, 25 April 1936.

   Jordan A. Schwartz, "Robert Lee Doughton," in *Dictionary of American Biography, Supplement Five* (New York: Charles Scribner's Sons, 1977) 190-191.

8. U.S. Congress, *Congressional Record* 80, 10583-10588.

9. U.S. Congress, *Congressional Record* 80, 10614-10615.

   Statutes at Large 49, 2041.

   New York Times, 21 June 1936, 30.

10. *The Public Papers and Addresses of Franklin D. Roosevelt, 1936* (New York: Random House, 1938), 238-240.

    New York Times, 4 July 1936, 1.

11. *Statutes at Large* 51, 564-615.

    Statutes at Large 52, 291-342.

    Statutes at Large 53, 685-738.

    Statutes at Large 54, 406-462.

12. *Congressional Record* 81, 4797.

    Congressional Record 84, 2992-2993.

13. *Congressional Record* 81, 4796-4797, 4799-4800.

    Congressional Record 84, 3055.

15. Svend Petersen, *A Statistical History of the American Presidential Elections* (New York: Frederick Ungar, 1963) 94-98.

    Richard M. Scammon (comp.), *America at the Polls: A Handbook of American Presidential Election Statistics, 1920-1964* (Pittsburgh: Univ. of Pittsburgh Press, 1965), 474-476.

16. Bruce A. Ragsdale and Kathryn A. Jacob (eds.), *Biographical Directory of the American Congress, 1774-1989* (Washington, D.C.: GPO, 1989), 632, 702, 721, 931, 1005, 1066, 1726, 1831, 2085.

    Congressional Quarterly, Inc., *Guide to U.S. Elections* (Washington, D.C., 1985), 633-634, 931, 936, 941, 946, 951.

    Kenneth C. Martis, *The Historical Atlas of United States Congressional Districts, 1789-1983* (New York: Macmillan, 1982), 166-173, 276.

America's Unprotected Scenic Corridors: The Quest for a National Policy

Helen Cozzetto and Don Cozzetto

OVERVIEW

One of the most important public policy issues facing Americans in the next two decades will be the effective management of scenic resources, vistas or corridors along the nation's roadways. Despite the fact that discussion surrounding scenic byways occupies an increasing amount of time on the political agenda at both state and national levels, precious little effort has been directed toward developing a comprehensive policy strategy to protect the country's scenic landscapes from the tremendous pressures exerted by development. This paper seeks to focus on the many issues of this problem as experienced through a series of three case studies at the state level. It is hoped that these case studies can provide a framework for a national policy concerning scenic byway corridor protection.

INTRODUCTION

Fascination with America's scenic beauty can be traced back to the days of Thomas Jefferson when he eloquently documented his excitement over landscape vistas that captured his imagination during repeated rural travels.[1] Two Hundred years later, the increasing use of the automobile coupled with a dramatic increase in domestic tourism, has translated into broad, severe land-use implications for all three levels of government. Efforts to properly protect and manage our scenic resources along picturesque roadways, are increasingly critical as more and more of us begin to explore and exert pressures on America's scenic landscapes. Today, tourism represents one of the top three industries in forty of the fifty states.[2] Sadly enough, however, the federal government as well as many state and local governments do not seriously consider the ramifications of this 37 billion dollar a year industry.[3] Almost daily we read newspaper articles of rural scenic landscapes being destroyed by an influx of development which hopes to capitalize on the "intrinsic values" that make these landscapes so special.

A recent example of this was brought forth in April 1991 by Minnesota State Senator Roger Moe who sponsored a new scenic byway bill. This does not necessarily mean that the good Senator is a champion of scenic corridor protection. Rather, it seems that Moe owns property in the northwest part of the state. Last summer, the state department of transportation 'rebuilt to upgrade' a highway near Moe's property and in the process destroyed trees, wetlands and indeed the very scenic character of the landscape. This first hand experience so angered the senator that he proposed a statewide standard for roads that mirrors standards enforced in the national forests.[4] The inherent dichotomy in this example, is that the scenic land corridor which so attracted the public in the first place, created such pressures of development and congestion, that it was destroyed by the 'improved' quality of the highway. As we have all witnessed, the zeal to develop and exploit a fragile scenic resource often has the effect of "killing the goose that laid the golden egg."[5]

In 1987, the Report of the President's Commission on the *American Outdoors*, recommended that; "Local and state governments create a network of scenic byways... and take action to protect these resources." This statement along with the explosive growth of the tourist industry, has encouraged a resurgence of interest in scenic byways at all levels of government.

In February 1989, the first legislation in fifteen years on scenic byways was introduced in the Senate by Senator Jay Rockefeller (D-WV) and in the House by Congressman James Oberstar (DFL-MN).[6] The bill directed the Secretary of Transportation to study many aspects of scenic byways including the introduction of a national system, designation and guideline criteria, economic impacts, safety issues, and inventory of existing national corridors. In October 1989, approval was given by Congress to examine the Scenic Byways Bill and one million dollars was provided for a yearlong study, which is now complete.

During one of his press announcements, Senator Rockefeller stated, "Preserving scenic beauty is one goal of a national scenic byway program but there's also a tremendous economic benefit." It is this statement that reinforces the economic development preservation dichotomy discussed above and why an assessment of existing scenic corridor protection was undertaken. If scenic byways in fact are a catalyst for the ever-growing tourist industry, it is vital that we know how to properly protect and manage all of our scenic resources that make this economic development so attractive.

Much research has been done on the effects of increased human activity on the environmental degradation of scenic resources. However, little research has been conducted on the larger issues of aesthetic degradation of scenic landscapes (referred to as corridors), along roadways. This paper assesses the successes and failures of scenic corridor protection in three state-designated scenic byways programs. These programs provide a cross-section of the country and representative of a ten case study thesis which assessed long-established scenic byway programs in the US.[7]

This research indicates that the scenic byway field is currently fragmented and that a need exists for a "holistic" approach to scenic corridor protection. The need for both research and specific policy action has recently been accelerated by Congress's inability to deal effectively with corridor protection. The 1991 Highway and Transportation Bill falls far short of the mark. Indeed, the Senate's version would effectively roll back many of the existing laws controlling "managed trashing" of interstate and primary roads, a move that may well affect scenic roads as well. It is the federal government's responsibility to ensure that scenic corridors are protected as a whole, while allowing state and local governments the flexibility needed to develop concrete policies and implementation strategies that are jurisdiction specific.

HISTORICAL OVERVIEW

In order for the reader to understand the need for a comprehensive management strategy aimed at protecting scenic corridors, it is important to consider current developments in light of historical antecedents.

The first parkways were constructed by state and municipal governments in the early 1890s and 1900s Examples include the Bronx River Parkway and the Westchester County Parkway.[8] Despite the fact that Congress passed legislation defining a national vision for parkways in 1916, the federal government did not implement the policy until 1929 when funds were appropriated for the construction of the Mount Vernon Parkway.[9] Probably the most famous parkway in the country, the Blue Ridge Parkway, was constructed under Roosevelt's New Deal administration.[10] The 1960s brought a renewed interest in the environment in general and scenic corridor protection in particular. President Johnson was a strong proponent of the 1965 Highway Beautification Act. He envisioned a comprehensive aesthetic program which included legislation concerning scenic roads, easements, and control of billboards along highways. Unfortunately, as with many innovative policy initiatives, the dollars appropriated by legislators fell far short of the intent of the visionaries who proposed the legislation.

Despite the fact that there have been renewed efforts by some politicians at the federal level—an example is Congressman Peter H. Kostmayer's bill titled "The American Landscape Protection Act of 1990"—as well as some private initiatives—The American Society of Landscape Architects' proposal to include aesthetics under conservation reserve objectives in the 1990 Farm Bill—the strategies aimed at scenic corridor protection are fragmented and oftentimes inconsistent with broader long-term political objectives. In addition, the increasing federal deficit has continued to limit discretionary spending in most areas other than defense.[11] This perpetual state of financial exigency has seriously constrained efforts at more comprehensive policies concerning corridor management.

A number of important beautification and land management initiatives have been undertaken over the years in many states. Three of these oldest programs include California, Maine, and Minnesota. These case studies attempt to highlight the significant events that have developed recently and to determine if there is any common foundation upon which a comprehensive national corridor management policy can be constructed.

CALIFORNIA

California has had a long history of land use conflicts between growth development and the protection of its scenic resources. The problem will be exacerbated by the prediction that the state's population will increase by an additional ten million by the year 2010.[12] How well the state will respond to this massive increase in demand upon its scenic resources base remains to be seen, but indications are that the population today takes seriously its commitment to a high quality of life standard. In 1990, this was evidenced by a plethora of environmental issues being considered by politicians, public administrators, interest groups, and the public writ-large. This acute awareness translates into public debate and fosters the "pure democracy" model of government through the use of public referenda.

Over the years, California has used a variety of land management tools to try and protect its scenic resources from indiscriminate development. Since the early 1930s when scenic easements were initiated to protect views and open space lands along highways (especially coastlines), the need to protect scenic corridors adjacent to roadways has been of continuing concern. In 1963 the legislature passed the State Scenic Highways Program to address this issue and "establish the State's responsibility for the protection and enhancement of California's natural beauty by identifying those portions of the state highway system which, together with the adjacent scenic corridors, require special scenic conservation treatment."[13]

Although the California Department of Transportation (Caltrans) administers all scenic highway programs, responsibility for specifics such as the designation and protection of the scenic corridor, rests with local government agencies of cities and counties. This decentralization component is important. In calling for a national policy on scenic byways we in no way infer that the federal government should be involved in micro managing specific jurisdictions. We believe that state and local agencies will welcome a national policy detailing specific standards and providing categorical grants as long as they maintain the autonomy to develop policies that are peculiar to their own geographic areas.

Caltrans's Perspectives

California's scenic highway program is characterized by locally developed tools such as general (comprehensive) plans, specific plans, and ordinances. State scenic highway regulations specify that cities and/or counties develop and implement scenic corridor protection programs to conform with state requirements.

These protection programs vary from one jurisdiction to another. In general, the degree of controls are at a level necessary to protect the scenic appearance of the corridor and to meet community goals. The protection measures can be in the form of regulations or policies in the local general plan or area plans.

The minimum requirements for a scenic protection program listed below have been part of the scenic highway program since 1963.

1. Regulation of land use and density of development
2. Detailed land and site planning
3. Control of outdoor advertising
4. Careful attention to and control of earth moving and landscaping 5. Regulation of design and appearance of structures and equipment.[14]

State scenic highway program regulations call for monitoring the local protection program and renewal of the official scenic designation every five years. Renewal is granted if local official and the Caltrans District Scenic Highway Coordinator concur that the protection program is being enforced. Those communities not in compliance have one year to meet standards or withdraw from the program. This tool can be effective, if diligently applied. However, enforcement at both the local and state level varies with the degree of interest in the program and the availability of funding.

Direct program costs at the state level are confined to a portion of the personnel costs for the program coordinator and for some district coordinators.

Caltrans considers public awareness and participation the most important tool in this program. The local scenic highway protection program should be prepared in cooperation with local citizens' committees, affected property owners, environmental groups and anyone else who would be impacted by the proposed designation. Ideally, these groups are involved at the earliest possible date to afford ample time for review and comment before official action is taken. Effective citizen participation will result in a protection program which generally meets local desires.

Corridor protection programs in officially designated state scenic highway corridors are subject to specific review by Caltrans. However, all general plan elements are reviewed by the department as part of the California Environmental Quality Act review process. Many general plans contain a scenic highway component, which is an optional element of the enabling legislation.

California has established a list of state highways eligible for scenic designation, but participation is strictly a local option. Caltrans feels that they should be partners in land-use/transportation decisions, but the state should not dictate local land use. Today the conflicts over growth control is an issue that affects scenic corridors and the scenic highway program. Those wishing stricter control over land use will see scenic highway designation as an aid. Those who wish to intensify local growth

MAINE

Maine's scenic highway program was initiated as a direct result of the 1965 Highway Beautification Act. In 1969 the Maine Scenic Highway Board was created and later restructured in 1972 under the Commissioner of Transportation.[15] The Commissioner, charged with establishing a scenic byway system, considers the following:

1. scenic value
2. safety aspects
3. economic implications
4. preservation of scenic value
5. compatibility with other national, regional and local conservation plans.[16]

Although a number of state statutes emphasize the protection of scenic beauty and the various land management tools to protect the scenic quality of its highway corridors, the primary purpose of the program today is considered in the context of economic development and tourism.

Maine is a strong Home Rule state.[17] The Departments of Transportation and Economic Development oversee land management issues but programs are administered and enforced through local planning boards and Conservation Commissions. This results in a wide variety of land management techniques being applied which presents problems in assessing each local jurisdiction's success rate.

Maine's Department of Transportation Perspective

Maine employs a wide variety of land management tools to protect its scenic resources. These include: zoning (both at the state and local levels), scenic area overlay districts, design review overlay techniques, highway/transportation overlay districts, special permits (use or density restrictions), buffers and set backs, architectural controls, sign controls, fee acquisition/leaseback, and wider than usual road right-of-ways. The Department of Transportation does not administer or manage many of these tools but concentrates its work on the design and maintenance of landscape forestry. Visual assessment techniques are part of the formal process and selective thinning is considered the department's specialty.

From the Department of Transportation's standpoint, there are two issues regarding administration and enforcement that concern them. The first is the lack of coordination between those trying to preserve and protect scenic corridors and timber companies who own large tracts of land bordering scenic roads. Many timber companies clear-cut forest crops without regard to the scenic aspects of the resource. Officials within the Maine Department of Transportation stress the need for a comprehensive orientation program for these companies. They express their frustration at trying to enhance aesthetic qualities along the state's roads only to have an adjacent parcel of land decimated. What is needed is a coordinated effort between private and public sector agencies aimed at the development of a unified land management strategy.[18]

The second problem for the Department of Transportation is the issue of growth along scenic corridors. Comprehensive planning at the county levels is often poorly coordinated with the state's overall objectives. This adds to the difficulty in retaining the existing character of the scenic corridors. Since 1968, Maine has had land management information on file but no specific, tangible legal standards, so that enforcement of standards has been uneven at best.

A related issue is the much publicized state of financial exigency affecting eastern seaboard states in general and Maine in particular.[19] This translates into a reduced commitment of scarce financial resources to scenic land management. When times are tough politicians have difficulty understanding that scenic resource protection is a high priority. The perfect analog is the traditional approach on large construction projects. When the budget is tight the first part of the project that gets cut is the landscape, because this approach views the landscape only as an afterthought or in fragmented terms which can be manipulated to suit the specific building construction.

Program Summary

Maine's scenic highway program has been in existence for a sufficient length of time that allows the Department of Transportation to pinpoint current difficulties and to predict future problems. At the present time, politicians view tourism on scenic roads as the primary vehicle to regional economy recovery. Yet, they are unwilling and probably unable to allocate the much needed resources to protect the scenic landscape. Private land trusts and community groups are struggling to protect small parcels of scenic lands in the state, but the Department of Transportation realizes that a comprehensive effort to protect scenic corridors must be initiated at state and federal levels in order to effectively protect these scenic resources.

Maine views a federal scenic byways program as a positive step toward protecting existing scenic resources. This is a departure from traditional highway thought which has been concerned only with infrastructure. The Department feels perhaps it is time to broaden its thinking and reassess the department's role in resource protection.

MINNESOTA

In 1924, the scenic North Shore Highway in Minnesota was opened to the motoring public. Meandering along the magnificent waters of Lake Superior, it remains one of the most spectacular scenic roads in the United States. Yet with all Minnesota's scenic management experience on roadways, it is perhaps surprising to learn that the state is only now in the process of consolidating an official scenic byways program.

Historically, Minnesota has been a leader in the area of innovation when it comes to scenic land management. Since the early 1950s the state has administered a scenic easement program dedicated to acquiring scenic lands adjacent to highways. The legislation establishing the program dates back to 1965.[20] Its main purpose was to preserve scenic lands in private ownership and control the proliferation of billboard and outdoor advertising. The need to further improve visual qualities along highways prompted the state legislature to initiate a new program in 1971 aimed at controlling and eliminating junk yards along public roads. These efforts were followed by various land use statutes which are related to highway projects including limited use permits, transfer of fee title lands, highway easements, and cooperative agreements with other pertinent agencies.[21]

In 1978, Minnesota began to devote considerable attention to its role in the development of the Great River Road. This federally assisted project encompassing ten states and two provinces along the Mississippi River, lends definitive proof to the fact that collaborative efforts between various levels of government and private agencies can culminate in a major success story. Minnesota regards this project as atypical of other scenic roads within the state because management and administrative issues are handled separately through the Minnesota Mississippi River Parkway Commission.

In 1986, as part of the State Transportation Act, the Minnesota legislature passed a new law promoting recreational enhancement along state scenic highways. The law called Highways In Recreation Areas (HIRA), dictates the coordination of highway construction and recreation opportunities between the Department of Transportation and the Department of Natural Resources. Cooperative interagency efforts have been specifically laid out, including the evaluation and designation of "unique and scenic" highway segments "to protect, interpret or enhance the visual, natural or cultural character of roadway corridors."[22]

Minnesota's Department of Transportation Perspective

Minnesota has recently established several programs related to scenic roads. These programs include:

1. Scenic Easement Program
2. Great River Road Program
3. Highways in Recreation Areas
4. North Shore Management Plan
5. De Facto Management Program

The goals and objectives of each program vary but all include a combination of scenic preservation, improvement of recreational opportunities and tourist-related economic development. The Great River Road program also lists historic preservation as one of its purposes.

Land management tools used specifically for scenic corridor protection are applied in the North Shore and De Facto programs. The Scenic Easement, Highways In Recreation Areas, and Great River Road programs do not use land management tools for this specific reason.

The Department of Transportation is the lead agency in the De Facto program. This program incorporates a cooperative effort with the Department of Agriculture Weed Inspectors. The Department of Transportation will also be the lead agency in the new Scenic Byways program. The North Shore program is overseen by counties and communities and the Great River Road program by the Mississippi River Parkway Commission and adjacent communities. The De Facto, Scenic Easement, and Great River Road programs are administered and enforced at the state level; the North Shore and Great River Road at both the county and local levels.

The following tools are used by Minnesota in scenic byway management:

1. The North Shore program employs comprehensive planning, local level zoning, special conservation or corridor districts and special purpose boards or authorities.

2. The Great River Road program employs local level zoning (billboards), sign control, conservation or scenic easements, wider than usual road right-of-way (paved shoulders), voluntary programs and special purpose boards or authorities.

3. The Scenic Easement program employs scenic area overlay districts, sign control, fee acquisition/leaseback, conservation or scenic easements and technical committees.

4. The De Facto program employs erosion and sediment controls, and wider than usual road right-of-way.

The Great River Road was chosen by the Department of Transportation for land management assessment because those responsible for the project have over ten years experience in the application of land management techniques. The following criteria was used for assessment purposes.

1. Fit local expectations; conduct local meetings and use results in route development guides.

2. Funnel funds through local agencies.
3. Incorporate a statewide advocacy group such as the Legislative Commission in the Great River Road.

Results indicated that fitting local expectations and incorporating a statewide advocacy group is considered very effective. Funneling funds through local agencies is considered only moderately effective. All three approaches lend themselves to ease of administration. Counties are charged with specific administrative responsibilities but work closely with state agencies as well as the Legislative Commission.

The Scenic Easement program was highly effective when it was initially implemented. However, the state's inventory of properties is not easily accessible, and so there has been a lack of continuity and follow-up in the program over time. The properties are still owned by the state but land uses have not been inventoried or monitored within recent years. There appears to be a real need to update this information especially in light of the fact that the program was such a major investment over 30 years ago.

Minnesota does not differentiate between the management of scenic byways with other land management programs and finds optimal effectiveness in programs where a combination of state agencies are working together on a project. Each agency has a vested interest in some phase of the project so that goal attainment and project completion are enhanced. Task forces are also effective in this sense and may have significant non-agency membership from the community. The Department of Transportation also feels that participation with local communities cannot be underscored.

In both the short and long-terms, issues of development and harvesting of natural resources are significant concerns for Minnesota's scenic roads programs. In the short-term, the development and adoption of the Scenic Byway system is a concern due to a changing political climate. In the long-run, the system's maintenance is a concern due to long-range financial constraints.

Program Summary

Minnesota's scenic byway protection issues differ from those states that have experienced overwhelming development pressures during the past twenty years. Nearly 27% of the state's land base is owned by the federal government,[23] so land-use issues outside the major urban centers, tend to focus on vegetation and wildlife management and resource harvesting.[24] Scenic protection does not seem to be a problem with public lands. Private land that has been critical to retain for scenic purposes, has often been bought by the state or placed under the scenic easement program.

Over the years, the Department of Transportation has worked extensively with visual analysis techniques for use on scenic corridors and has recently developed a comprehensive Visual Impact Assessment Process which is legally grounded on various aesthetic and environmental laws.[25] Although this process is still in its infancy, it offers many exciting possibilities for cataloging and assessing impacts on scenic corridors which can be used to decide important protection issues.

The Transportation Department has also expressed interest in setting up a taxonomy for typical landscapes.[26] This recognizes the need to go beyond the current emphasis on spectacular landscapes to include land and water forms unique to specific regions. For example, the prairie landscape is often viewed as unattractive by local residents. However, many tourists find it fascinating. Equally important is the fact that these types of landscapes are bowing to the pressures of development and so are also rapidly disappearing.

During the 1988 draft stage of the new Highways In Recreational Areas program, the greatest percentage of comments referred to a need for more public and interagency cooperation on all scenic highway projects. These include more streamlined administrative procedures, a concerted effort at retrofit and enhancement of existing facilities, and more effective highway signing.[27] It remains to be seen if Minnesota will be successful in its new cooperative vision of scenic protection. To date, their track record has been one of the best in the country.

CONCLUSION

The three case studies presented above highlight some of the positive and negative aspects of initiatives concerning scenic byway/corridor management at the state level. Appendix A depicts a table of the breakdown of land management tools used by all ten states in the original thesis and highlights the most frequently used across the country.

Let us now turn our attention to another state which has no scenic byways program in place at this time. At present, North Dakota is skeptical of any federal involvement in scenic byways programs, viewing them as just more lost revenue for construction and maintenance programs.[28] However, the recent influx of Canadian travelers and various film images are impacting the state's tourism industry and the state is trying to 'cash in' on this windfall, which brings us back to the dichotomy discussed earlier in this paper.

Until recently, many Mid-West states have conjured up images of bald prairie and raging blizzards. But a resurgence in 'western interest' displays a tremendous beauty of the land and a rich history attached to the opening up of the Dakota territory. Even so problems associated with the lack of proper regional planning are eroding some of this roadside beauty, especially near urban centers. This problem is now beginning to surface on the Lewis and Clark trail leading into the Fort Abraham Lincoln State Park outside Bismarck. Billboards, residential and commercial development and lack of protection for river bottom lands have resulted in creeping destruction of the scenic resources' along this roadway. Some progress has been made to establish scenic easements along critical viewsheds leading into Fort Lincoln but increasingly this pressure has come from the public. In a recent public meeting on the future needs of the park, "acquiring lands and scenic easements to protect park integrity," was listed as a top priority requiring immediate attention by all of the public participants. Over 60 people attended this meeting and represented a wide range of special interest groups.[29] Interestingly enough, the Highway Department will have nothing to do with this initiative, even though the road is considered a scenic road of national importance and is managed on both the state and federal levels. Their view is that scenic byway programs and corridor protection are considered a low state priority and funnels money from more important interstate road development and maintenance.[30] Even the Tourism Department, which is charged to promote the beauty of the state openly endorses the use of billboard advertising in its promotional campaigns and uses a mini-billboard to display its mission statement.

At the beginning of this paper, we indicated a need for a comprehensive national policy with respect to the very important subject of landscape degradation along America's unprotected roadways. As evidenced by the lack of cohesiveness in this field, it is increasingly obvious that the federal government must take a proactive role in this regard.

Now that the interstate highway system is almost complete, Congress has turned its attention to what has been termed "highway demonstration projects."[31] Several key politicians have benefited handsomely from this new focus. The Senate Appropriations Chairman Robert Byrd secured $137 million for his home state of West Virginia,[32] David Bonior received $3.9 million for a bicycle trail in Michigan, Representative Lehman, and Chairman of the House Transportation Appropriations Subcommittee received approval for an $18.6 million project to revitalize the Biscayne Boulevard in Miami.[33] This exercise in pork barrel politics is characterized by Francis Francois, Executive Director of the American Association of State Highway and Transportation Officials as "nothing more than the congressman's ability to get money for his district."[34]

The 1992 Transportation Bill, currently the subject of great debate on the floors of Congress, falls far short of dealing with the realities of the situation. On July 10, 1991 the House Appropriations Subcommittee on Transportation approved a $14.2 billion bill for the transportation department for fiscal 1992. However, on August 1 an embarrassed group of Democratic House leaders were forced to pull the five-year 153.5 billion highway bill. The bone of contention is the proposed five cent a gallon gasoline tax. Many members of Congress oppose the tax because they claim that it is regressive, affecting in a disproportionate way low and middle income Americans.[35] Congress needs to get its act together. Implementation of the following recommendations would greatly assist state and local governments in their efforts at scenic corridor protection:

1. Develop a series of national minimum standards similar to those currently in place for wetlands protection. Specifics would include:

    - the designation of specific highways as scenic.
    - development of comprehensive scenic corridor plans by all state highway agencies. Municipal and county governments would then be required to conform to the state plan.
    - close loopholes and develop regulations governing outdoor advertising, regional and site planning, and landscaping.
    - specific regulations prohibiting obstructions or clear cutting in scenic vistas.

2. Implement the five cent fuel tax. One cent of the tax to be targeted toward corridor protection and transferred to the state level.[36]

3. All demonstration projects be considered in the broader context of corridor protection.

4. Establish a joint committee to ensure a coordinated effort at policy implementation—i.e., federal and state representatives from key departments such as transportation, environment, and tourism would constitute the committee.

None of us would be so naive as to proclaim a "quick fix" for the aesthetic protection of America's highway corridors. The issues involve politics, and the complexity of the situation is exacerbated by the number and levels of governments involved. One thing is clear, however. The 1990s is no place for continued political rhetoric and electoral calculus. Policy guidelines and the appropriate funding must come from an informed federal government. Members of Congress must act quickly and without favoritism before the damage to our scenic corridors becomes irreparable.

Helen E. Cozzetto is Manager of Planning and Development for the North Dakota State Park system. She holds degrees in photography and architecture and has recently completed a Master of Landscape Architecture from Virginia Polytechnic Institute & State University.

Dr. Don A. Cozzetto is Assistant Professor and Director of Graduate Programs in the Department of Political Science at the University of North Dakota. His Ph.D. is in public administration from Virginia Polytechnic Institute & State University.

NOTES

1. See Edwin M. Betts and H. B. Perkins, *Thomas Jefferson's Flower Garden at Monticello*, (Charlottesville, VA: University Press of Virginia, 1986).
2. G. M. Bastarsche, "Scenic Highways Targeted," *American Automobile Association Fact Sheet*, Summer 1989.
3. Remarks by Undersecretary Rockwell A. Schnabel before the Scenic Byways Conference, American Recreation Coalition, Washington, DC, November 6, 1989.
4. See "Moe's Scenic Highway Bill Strikes Sparkes In Hearing," *Grand Forks Herald*, April 18, 1991, B-3.
5. "Development Paints Grim Vista at Shenandoah," *The Washington Post*, October 7, 1989 and "Congressmen Seeking Study of Shenandoah Battlefields," *The Washington Post*, December 9, 1989.
6. Bills S 432 and HR 1087.
7. Helen Cozzetto, *The Status of Corridor Protection Along Scenic Byways*, Unpublished Master of Landscape Architecture Thesis, Virginia Polytechnic Institute and State University, Blacksburg, VA, 1990.
8. David R. Levin, "Scenic Corridors," *Highway Research Record #166*, (Washington, DC: Highway Research Board, 1967).
9. Domenico Annese, "The Impact of Parkways on Development in Westchester County, New York City and the Metropolitan New York Region," *Parkways: Past, Present and Future*, (Boone, NC: Appalachian Consortium Press, 1987).
10. Harley E. Jolley, *The Blue Ridge Parkway*, (Knoxville, TN: University of Tennessee Press, 1969).
11. See *The 1991 Budget in Brief*, Washington: Office of Management and Budget.
12. Irving Schiffman, *Alternative Techniques for Managing Growth*, (Berkeley, CA: University of California Institute of Government Studies, 1990).
13. California Streets and Highway Code-Div. 1 Ch.2 Art 2.5
14. Ibid.
15. Maine Department of Transportation In-House document—January 20, 1975.
16. Ibid. p. 1.
17. See Donald Hagman and Julian C. Juergensmeyer. *Urban Planning and Land Development Control Law*. (St. Paul, MN: West Publishing Company, 1986) pp. 53-54.
18. Telephone interview with Mr. Clyde Walton, Landscape Architect for the Maine Department of Transportation, March 20, 1990.
19. The reader may recall that the Governor and Legislature could not agree on a fiscal 1991 budget. The result was that Maine's government infrastructure virtually shut down for two weeks in July.
20. Minnesota Statute &173.04
21. *Highways in Recreation Areas*, (St. Paul, MN: Minnesota Department of Transportation, September 1988).
22. *HIRA*, note 20 supra, p. 3.
23. *HIRA*, note 20 supra, p. 4.
24. *Corridor Management Plan*, supra.
25. *Visual Quality for EIS Processes*, (St. Paul, MN: Department of Transportation; Environment Services Section, 1989).
26. Telephone interview with Catherine Thayer, Senior Planner for Minnesota Department of Transportation, March 20, 1990.
27. *HIRA*, supra, p. 25.
28. Phone conversation with Norlyn Schmidt—North Dakota Department of Transportation Planning Division; Bismarck, ND, Oct. 16, 1991.
29. North Dakota Parks and Tourism Department: Fort Abraham Lincoln State Park Advisory Board Survey, May 22, 1991.
30. Phone conversation, note 28 supra.
31. See Mike Mills, "Lawmakers Lard Highway Bill with $6.8 Billion in Projects," *Congressional Quarterly*, July 27, 1991.
32. See Lawrence J. Haas, "Bird's Big Budget Stick," *National Journal*, February 9, 1991.
33. "House Travels Favorite Road To Funding Local Highways," *Congressional Quarterly*, Vol. 49, No. 28, July 13, 1991.
34. Ibid, p. 1884.
35. David S. Cloud, "House Dispute Over Gas Tax Puts Highway Bill on Hold," *Congressional Quarterly*, August 3, 1991.
36. The tax was estimated to increase annual revenues by approximately $6 billion. $1.2 billion would be allocated to scenic corridor protection.

Historic Resorts: Rediscovery of an American Legacy

Judy Byrd Brittenum

Abstract

As America watched its role as an industrialized nation unfold, the orchestration of resort development and the preservation of natural scenery counterbalanced the impact of the new lifestyle. In the period between 1875 and 1920, the intrigue of the resort community fueled the park movement and the preservation of outdoor space and natural scenery. This paper will explore the particular relationships between two cities, Hot Springs, Arkansas and Asheville, North Carolina, as examples of resort communities that played key roles. It will investigate the social and cultural reasons for this genre to command such an important place in America's environmental and conservation movement.

The glory of the leading men often overshadowed the cast that provided the artistic, design and technical support for resort development. Often, little is known about the input of the design professionals who plan these places. At the turn of this century, Colonel Samuel Fordyce in Hot Springs and George Washington Vanderbilt in Asheville, embarked upon independent ventures which attempted to bring Man, Health and Nature back into balance. Both of these men assembled the best of America's design professionals to ensure that their ventures would be successful. Richard Morris Hunt, George Mann, Eugene John Stern, and John Lawrence Mauran were the architects and Fredrick Law Olmsted and Jens Jensen, the landscape architects, who contributed to the unique architectural significance of these towns. They would design a classical heritage in cultural and physical resort development which would serve these towns even until today.

Vanderbilt and Fordyce provided the masses with models of elegance (Biltmore House and the Fordyce Bathhouse), entertained guests not only in their opulent palaces but also in their rustic lodges, contributed to the establishment of forestry programs and enabled such present day treasures as Pisgah National Forest, the Blue Ridge Parkway, and Hot Springs National Park to become realities. The paper will examine relationships between the men and their entourage and those impacts on tourism today.

Introduction

This is the story of two mountain towns that rose to prominence as health resorts by the late 1800s. These two, Asheville, North Carolina, and Hot Springs, Arkansas, flourished longer than most of their counterparts and still attract travelers today. Furthermore, the landscapes that surround these places were catalytic models for the preservation of natural scenery and fueled the park and outdoor recreation movements in the United States.

While health resorts were usually visited first for medical reasons, they often became Meccas for the wealthy. The adjacent scenery and landscape contributed visually and aesthetically to their mystic. The popularity of this landscape encouraged the restoration and preservation of these natural treasures and provided economic, social, and cultural reasons to maintain them (Cohen, 1978, 218; Pigram, 1980, 520). The premise of this paper is that today's tourism and continued economic and cultural development in Asheville and Hot Springs is largely due to certain key socially and financially prominent individuals who had selected the towns as their homes by the turn of the century. Additionally these men orchestrated acquisition there and provided protection for perpetuation of that natural legacy. (Swaim, 1981, 42)

George Washington Vanderbilt in Asheville and Samuel Wesley Fordyce in Hot Springs adopted these towns as their permanent homes and brought with them a more affluent lifestyle, an entourage of visitor-friends, financial support for regional development and their own personal interests in the environment surrounding these resorts. Without their particular efforts to preserve the native beauty of the adjacent land, the context of these towns might have been largely lost. Using Vanderbilt as a well-known example of a man who helped to develop and preserve Asheville first as his home and later as a national landscape, this paper will compare Samuel Fordyce's same influence in Hot Springs. This comparison of the two city fathers will reveal a historic pattern that might be applied to other turn of the century health resorts which are still viable tourist attractions today.

George Vanderbilt and Samuel Fordyce dreamed dreams and then executed them with flourish. Today there are certain residuals which can be directly attributed to the influence of these men and provide a continuum for tourism today. These are:

1. Unique, professionally designed architecture, both building and landscape, of which both private and public examples exist; and

2. Parks and other outdoor, set-aside land including natural corridors, parkways and forests. (Gunn, 1988)

To expand the idea that these men provided models for viable historic resort development, some basic tenets of tourism must first be examined, then a brief summary of the existing conditions at these towns when Vanderbilt and Fordyce arrived and a look at the Victorian times in which they lived.

Tourism Planning

Today successful tourism must address the social, cultural, and economic needs of a resort. Most already have unique visual qualities, whether architecture or landscape. Future development, however, can have negative impact as well as a positive one. In order to ensure the viability of these inherent characteristics, protection of the physical and cultural resources as well as promotion of non-intrusive recreation opportunities must be secured. It is often the influential efforts of key individuals that saves these resorts from the effects of poor development: homogeneity and cultural dilution, economic strain, and physical encroachment. (Gunn, 1988)

When historic resorts are protected or sensitively enhanced, they retain an appreciable amount of the original character that made them significant. Unique sustainable architecture and landscape is most often at the heart of good tourism, planning and attention to incorporating local culture provides an interchange between the two.

The selection of key social, cultural and economic conditions at the place is critical. Unique architecture can be both public and private. Landscape may relate to issues of recreation, visual scenery, or urban adjacency. Cultural conditions link the native and visitor and may involve both art and craft. The basic understanding of the historical context of a region and the particular eras which impacted them are often the most crucial increments of information when linking the these social cultural and economic conditions together.

Asheville and Hot Springs Before Vanderbilt and Fordyce

Asheville and Hot Springs, both located near historic Indian lands,, developed partially as early trail stops. Asheville lay on part of a road which originated in South Carolina and ran through North Carolina to Tennessee. Called "The Land of Sky" in promotional literature, Asheville developed a regional reputation when people found that cool, summer mountain air worked as a curative for consumption and malaria. Hot springs, with greater trail claims as part of the Hernando Desoto route, was perhaps first known for its intrinsic geological resources. It was, in fact, the "Valley of the Vapors" which drew the Indians and the famous explorer band to the healing hot waters long before the permanent settlers came.

The travelers visiting the two towns were quite different. The more affluent Southerners traveling to Asheville could afford to gather their children, servants and goods and move to higher ground for the duration of the summer. These visitors came to prevent illness as well as cure it. In Hot Springs the ill sought the healing waters and came in many circumstances. The position of these resorts was to provide basic accommodations for guests while they sought good health. Many of the permanent inhabitants scurried to make quick money or provide recreational, tavern-like entertainment. Others looked with a long eye at these dallying pursuits and saw more opportunity in building a broader base on which the communities could grow. (Eubank, 1936)

In Asheville primitive shelters and then taverns, like Alexander I's, had existed along the Buncombe Turnpike for quite some time. These taverns gave way to the larger wood-frame or brick inn. The Eagle Hotel, built in 1814, and the Buck Hotel, built in 1825, were some of the earliest. The popular Swannanoa Hotel came along in 1879 and other more elaborate hotels followed. (Swain, 1981, 35)

Some of these hotels cost as much as $200,000 and were kept open the entire year. "It was the day of family-style hostelries in Asheville and the surrounding valleys, where ladies wore dresses of muslin and crinoline that swept the floor, and no gentleman would think of removing his coat while toiling up Beaucatcher Mountain." (*Asheville Citizen*)

Hot Springs, too, had established a hotel and tourist trade based on its health resort image. "In 1820, Joseph and Nancy Mellard built the first of the many hotelries that before the end of the century would distinguish Hot Springs as a city of hotels." (Brown, 1982, 12) This was quite a remarkable venture since Hot Springs only had 84 people living in the township at that time. The thermal springs soon brought much business to the early health resort. The Hale Bath House and Hotel began the first of many visitor-related developments. The Rector and Stidham's Hotel were promoted as having conveniences for warm-bathing for invalids. These more primitive places were eventually replaced by luxurious hotels and eleven separate Spanish Renaissance bathhouses, making up what was then and is now called "Bathhouse Row." (Scully, 1966)

The imported inhabitants of the two towns soon outnumbered the locals. The citizens became more accepting of "different habits, religions, morals, dress, likes, and dislikes and speech patterns." (Brown, 1979) The tolerance of new and different customs subsequently influenced change when many rural South towns resisted it. Asheville was eventually to be even more greatly influenced by Vanderbilt's continental friends. Hot Springs too had an influx of wealthy outsiders. Due to Samuel Fordyce's influence in getting the government to build the new Army and Navy Hospital there and the growing Hot Springs Reservation lessees, many outside medical and military personnel arrived to oversee the business there.

The Victorian Era Influences On Resort Development

The Gilded Age was a term used to

describe the culture of the newly rich during the period of about 1870 to 1916. The industrial growth that began in the early 1800s. and boomed again after the Civil War gave rise to many new products and production methods. Inventions such as the telephone, the phonograph, the electric light, the first skyscraper, the automobile and the airplane provided opportunities for incredible economic change in America.

The social and cultural changes, however, differed greatly between the North and the South. The South remained mostly rural and poor while the North flourished. The untaxed, Northern wealthy were always seeking amusing ways to spend their money. For example, The Four Hundred was a group of inner-circle New York socialites designated thus by Mrs. William Backhouse Astor because that was the number she could hold comfortably in the ballroom of her New York brownstone. They were regulated by dogma controlling such trivialities as not "letting two white or brown sauces follow each other in succession" in a meal or not serving "truffles twice in that dinner." (Vanderbilt, 1989, 98) New York society, on the other hand, unconventionally had been known to distribute party cigarettes rolled in $100 bills, held banquets where guests ate on horseback in grand ballrooms, and clad their dogs in $15,000 diamond collars. (Vanderbilt, 1989, 263) There was simply too much money that abounded, and there was no end in sight to the extravagant spending. At the same time the average pay for a worker in the United States was about $495 a year, and only one family in twenty made more than $3,000 a year. (Gustavus, 1939, 164) This was truly the Gilded Age, for some.

By the late 1880s, the rich were interested in getting away from the cold Northern winters and in protecting themselves from disease; the only commodity their money could not buy was good health. Newport, Rhode Island and Saratoga, New York had been major vacation colonies of the wealthy until then. (Paige, 1987) The move to warm, southern climates came about the time The Jekyl Island Club was formed. An initial group of 53 of the wealthiest men in the world hired noted landscape architect H. W. S. Cleveland to master plan their Georgia island community. Vanderbilt's older brother, William K. Vanderbilt, was a charter member of this club. (Mann, 1990, 7)

The major attraction for the club was its isolation. Hunting, fishing and boating were some amusements the guests enjoyed rather than the old social pastimes in New York. The artisan water there was purported to be as health-giving tonic. (Mann, 1990, 8) Now that they were comfortable with the civilization they had provided for themselves, the rich had begun to retrace their steps back to the wilderness.

Vanderbilt and Fordyce As Catalytic Models

Vanderbilt and Fordyce both indirectly and directly influenced the resort communities of Asheville and Hot Springs to become the tourist attractions they are today. Without a doubt, the natives who before took their home environment for granted began to look differently at those resources when the affluent began to arrive there. The influx of travelers brought a new sense of pride to the towns as the effect of the rich was evidence of the permanency of their new found prosperity. Even later, when other visitors no longer came for just health reasons, they continued to be drawn by the architecture, open land and scenery which contributed to the sense of place of each.

While monetary constraints and the personalities of Vanderbilt and Fordyce were quite different, nevertheless, it is easy to recognize that their business and personal interests, their visions about the quality of life, and their dreams for their adopted hometowns interrelate both with each other and with the previously outlined tenets of tourism. By examining first Vanderbilt and then Fordyce, it can more easily be understood how they embarked upon independent ventures which attempted to bring Man, Health, and Nature back into balance.

George Washington Vanderbilt

George Washington Vanderbilt, the youngest of William H. Vanderbilt's eight children was a "gentle youth, more serious and studious than his older siblings and something of a mother's boy." (Auchincloss, 1989, 58) He was dark, frail of build and shy. While his older brothers and sisters calculated ways to enter proper New York society, he read, studied philosophy, became fluent in eight foreign languages, and engaged in other intellectual pursuits. (Vanderbilt, 1989, 271)

The grandson of two opposing types, Cornelius "The Commodore" Vanderbilt, a unrelenting shipping and railroad tycoon, and his mother's father, a Dutch Reform minister, the young Vanderbilt was intent on handling his money and soul carefully. Writing in his diary at age 13, he entered this item:

> I don't think I have spent today as I should have done. I have trusted too much in my own ability and not enough in Jesus. (Auchincloss, 1989, 59)

The well-intended young Vanderbilt must have been influenced greatly by his extravagant family though. On their way up in New York society, they had been known to spend as much as $250,000 on one party and had often hired prominent architects to design sumptuous estates costing as much as seven million dollars. (Vanderbilt, 1989, 121; 188) But, after all, it was his grandfather The Commodore who, when he died, had more money in his estate than was held in the United States Treasury. George Vanderbilt's father more than doubled that figure. (Vanderbilt, 1989, 54)

Vanderbilt dedicated himself to a quality lifestyle in his adulthood. Not particularly interested in the societal games of his family, he was able to envision himself a gentleman land owner. In fact, in 1886 shortly after his mother and he came to the Battery Park Hotel in Asheville on a vacation, he began purchasing land for a mountain retreat.

Vanderbilt was to build a permanent estate which would become the hallmark for Asheville's future tourism trade. His home, The Biltmore, certainly stands as a significant architectural, feat, but the landscape which surrounds this residence probably gives as much credence to the building itself and to George Vanderbilt's part in developing Asheville. Vanderbilt sought the finest architect and landscape architect he knew, Richard Morris Hunt and Fredrick Law Olmsted, and commenced an effort which would catapult both Asheville and him into national history.

Basing the Biltmore Estate on the European model of land management, Vanderbilt began to buy all of the land that his eye could see from his new home site. This land would eventually become over 100,000 acres and include Mount Pisgah. He and architect Richard Morris Hunt planned his home to be one of the grandest in America. (Ward, 1989)

The residents of nearby Asheville had mixed feelings about the indomitable Mr. Vanderbilt and the other new residents and visitors who arrived almost daily. Some felt that the town would be marred by the influx of more people; others accepted the changes and decided to make the best of it in their own way. In his attempt to purchase all the land that he could see from his hilltop home, Vanderbilt gave an opening for humorist Bill Nye who lived at the Swannanoa Hotel to remark that the Vanderbilt mansion "commands a fine view of any place." (*Asheville Citizen*)

Vanderbilt continued his architectural influence in Asheville in other ways. While he was establishing the Biltmore Estate, Vanderbilt invested approximately 65% of the capital in the Kenilworth Inn, a competitor of the Battery Park Hotel. This luxurious hotel was to be destroyed by fire soon after its opening but was quickly replaced and is still in use as a sanatorium. Vanderbilt, seeking housing for the support facilities of his vast empire, established Biltmore Village at the gate of the grounds of the Biltmore. It would be many years before this small community would become a retail tourist attraction. Nevertheless, the attention to contiguous design, repeating the image of a English village nestled within Fredrick Law olmsted's romantic landscape at the Biltmore would later prove an appropriate frontispiece for the tourist-visited Biltmore home. Vanderbilt was instrumental, too, in developing the town Victoria and had five villas designed there which could house affluent, long-term Asheville visitors and their servant staff. While only one villa remains today, a collection of historic buildings in Victoria and Asheville employed the services of the Vanderbilt resident architect, Richard Sharpe Smith and the landscape architecture firm, Olmsted and Sons. (Swain, 1989; Beveridge, 1987, 109)

Without Vanderbilt's influence, none of this extended landscape would probably exist. The second influence that can be attributed directly to the model George Vanderbilt represents is his creation of a regional landscape. The parks, outdoor recreation corridors, and open land which remain today read like a Who's Who in national land acquisition: the first forestry school in the United States, Pisgah National Forest, and land which is now a part of the Blue Ridge Parkway. Vanderbilt borrowed from the Jekyl Island retreat idea when he built the isolated Buck 'Springs Lodge and Shut-In Trail near the summit of Mount Pisgah. The Shut-in Trail, running from the Biltmore grounds to the rustic-style, timber lodge (actually a compound of four buildings) was the focus of one humorous story. (Baldwin, 1991)

Vanderbilt did not believe the car a practical invention; his wife challenged him to admit that it was if she could get a car up Mount Pisgah. Imagine his surprise, after arriving at the lodge on horseback one day, to find the car awaiting him. Somehow, Mrs. Vanderbilt had managed to have the car driven, pulled and pushed over rugged, almost impassable terrain to the lodge. That same Shut-In Trail is a part of the Appalachian Trail System today. (Brower, 1978)

Strange that Vanderbilt, who had left the bustle of New York for his mountain retreat at Asheville, had to build yet another retreat. The hunting and outdoor recreation trend of the times had probably prompted him to construct the retreat for his wealthy friends who came to the Asheville mountains to get away from their urban homes and had found only splendor at The Biltmore.

Samuel Wesley Fordyce

From his birth Samuel Wesley Fordyce embraced life fully. The son of a minister and the oldest of eleven children, his Ohio home was the headquarters for Methodist circuit riders. There were often four to six at a time visiting and he, like Vanderbilt, made an individual identity statement for himself. Unlike the retiring Vanderbilt, Fordyce's youth was filled with unpredictable, boy-like pranks. By the age of sixteen he was sent away to school in Pennsylvania and then, after yet another episode, to even another school. (Fordyce, 1919)

Those two and a half years provided experiences which would change his attitude toward life forever. In the fall of 1858, he witnessed the historic Abraham Lincoln/Stephen A. Douglas debate. He became acquainted with the future president when Lincoln took time to play with the boys during the breaks in his schedule there. Later, on Fordyce's trip home from that institution, he stopped in Chicago and was permitted to spend time with the Illinois delegation when they declared Lincoln as their candidate for president. Fordyce arrived home in Senecaville a changed young man and went to work for his father who at that time had become director of the Central Ohio Railroad. (Fordyce, 1919)

Fordyce's life was soon interrupted by the Civil War, and he helped to organize the 1st Ohio Volunteer Cavalry. Serving the Union Army at the battles of Murfreesboro, Chickamuga, Shiloh and Perryville, Kentucky, he gained a reputation for valor. For example, he was wounded three times and was captured three times, but never served a day of imprisonment due to courageous escapes. (Fordyce, 1919)

It was during this time when he met his future wife, Susan Chadick,1 also the daughter of a Methodist clergyman but a daughter of the South as well. According to stories, Colonel Fordyce was in command of a district in Northern Alabama, and it was his duty to secure the lines. He met his bride-to-be after her father slipped across the Union lines to visit his family for a time. He was pursued by the Union soldiers, and Miss Chadick, in a hurry to protect her father's flee, accidently shot herself in the hand. It was Colonel Fordyce who came to call and express his regrets about the incident. After the end of the war, they were married, and the Fordyce's moved to Huntsville, Alabama, where Colonel Fordyce gained much respect and mutual love from the citizens of his new home. Fordyce, unlike many Northerners of that time, worked diligently to restore the economy of the South through his business, the Fordyce and Rison Bank. (Fordyce, 1919)

Unfortunately, Colonel Fordyce was beleaguered with postwar ill health due to sustained exposure, long duty and wounds. By late 1872, he was diagnosed as having six months to live. Leaving his wife and two children with her family, he took his doctor's advise and went alone to Hot Springs for a final chance at recovery.

The rough stagecoach ride brought him into Hot Springs to the only proper hotel in existence, one which was made of only planks and rough paper. (One of the proprietors, S. H. Stitt, had been a young man in Nashville when he met Fordyce the first time and provided him a cot on which to sleep during the Civil War.) Fordyce could not leave the crude Hot Springs bath house for two weeks as his weight had dropped from 175 to 120 pounds. Hot water was brought to him to drink and bathe in. Three months later, Fordyce had gained 20 pounds, was eating again and able to return to Alabama. (Fordyce, 1919)

Fordyce's gratitude for his new-found health challenged him to come back to Hot Springs. He wished to promote the city in order that others would know of its restorative waters. Using the same courageous spirit and energy which had served him during the war and during his illness, he moved his family to Hot Springs and concentrated on building it to national spa recognition. With Stitt, he was to build the palatial 300 room Arlington Hotel and himself pioneered the gas, electric light and water companies, and then the street railway system. (Scully, 1966) Later when his personal business empire, the Cotton Belt Railroad, took him physically away from the spa city, he would live in a grand French Chateau style home in St. Louis but still remain a resident of Hot Springs. (Savage, 1987; Fordyce, 1919) In 1904 he built a 18 room log home on 1,200 acres which he called "The Cabin" and to which he returned every Spring until his death in 1916.

John Fordyce often substituted for his father in business matters during this time. As Samuel Fordyce's oldest son, he would also become a major player in Hot Springs' development. Recognized nationally as an inventor, Desoto historian, and accomplished engineer, it was only after his father died and he had inherited "The Cabin" that he moved to Hot Springs to help carry on the Fordyce legacy there.

Samuel Fordyce influenced Hot Springs's development in the same two ways that Vanderbilt influenced Asheville development. Remaining today are significant architectural buildings, a grand hotel, and a national landscape which includes Hot Springs National Park and the Quachita National Forest. The Fordyce Bathhouse, now the interpretive center for Hot Springs National Park, and the Arlington Hotel are perhaps the most famous architecturally, but the old Fordyce home, "The Cabin," built in 1904, is an architectural wonder of the city little known today.

Secluded, the home retains approximately fifteen acres of its original 1,200 acre forest land. Like Vanderbilt's Buck Spring Lodge, it is also an example of a wilderness retreat. The 400 remaining acres of the Fordyce grounds are now a part of the Hot Springs National Park. The government also owns outlying site amenities as the water wheel which brought early electricity and water to the house, a lake, boat house, and other significant, Fordyce designed structures. The property grounds are laid out sensitivity by Fordyce for he knew first hand the restrictions of grades and site after supervising the construction of 24,000 miles of railroads from St. Louis to Texas.

Mr. Fordyce hired professional architects for his projects when he could. Architect John Lawrence Mauran of St. Louis designed "The Cabin" and George Mann and Eugene John Stern designed the Fordyce Bathhouse. Fordyce had a keen appreciation of landscape architecture too. He was interested in the manner in which the engineers would plot the streets of the town and the mountain roads adjacent to Bathhouse Row. Fordyce said that he knew that "modern" landscape architects strived for the effects which he had adapted from necessity in his railroad building days, and he oversaw the road building in Hot Springs so that it too would follow those same design ethics. (Fordyce, 1919) Fordyce's involvement in Hot Springs went well beyond the city limits for he had single-handedly brought about the most significant happening in Hot Springs history.

In 1832 the United States Government had set aside land for themselves for the first time when they designated the Hot springs Reservation. However, the men who were drawn initially to this unique area began to make leases and claim its natural resources for themselves. Finally, in 1876 the Supreme Court established a commission "to survey the reservation, to lay out the town and to consider the claims of the local residents and to reserve certain portions of the four sections, including the Hot Springs and Hot Springs Mountain as a Permanent Reservation." (Scully, 1966, 31)

Fordyce states in his autobiography that he believed that the most beneficial thing he had done in his life was to help bring about the passage of the bill that established that commission and a subsequent bill which set aside the mountain landscape adjacent to the Hot Springs corridor. Having known President Grant since his generalship in the Civil War, Fordyce went to Washington to help the

Arkansas delegation get the bill passed. At about three in the morning, this former union officer managed to see President Grant and persuade him to sign it. This bill was probably the last signed by Grant before he left office. It took another attempt to set aside over half of the mountainous terrain which surrounded the urban Hot Springs Creek. (Fordyce, 1916) This woodland and the land around "The Cabin" remain today as examples of the few old growth forests left in the United States.

Additionally, Samuel Fordyce's son, John, continued his father's impact on the forested area around Hot Springs by working to establish the Quachita National Forest. As honorary highway commissioner for the Arkansas Highway commission, he was instrumental in securing Blue Star Memorial Highway designation for part of the state road system as well as designing Highway 5 from Little Rock to Hot Springs as a parkway.

In 1909, Fordyce, acting through the Hot Springs Water Company and Railway Company, established Hot Springs Golf and Country Club. This club was one of the first U.S. golf courses with grass greens in this country and was devised to serve hotel guests in the town as well as city residents. Fordyce did not stop at outdoor recreation but built the Hot Springs Opera House as well. He invited many distinguished stars of the day like Lillian Russell. (Scully, 1966) Like Vanderbilt's Buck Springs Lodge and Shut-In Trail, Samuel Fordyce had a trail of his own which linked "The Cabin" with the Fordyce Bathhouse and the national park lands in downtown Hot Springs.

During the time the Fordyce's lived and directed much of the activity in Hot Springs, two professional landscape architects and a landscape engineer worked there. In 1890 Fredrick Law Olmsted consulted on initial site plans for Bathhouse Row and the adjacent Army and Navy Hospital grounds. Mr. Olmsted visited the park himself on his way to what would be his last trip to the Biltmore. (Olmsted, 1895) Those preliminary plans were probably not entirely his own however because Mr. Olmsted's health failed almost immediately thereafter. Later the noted Chicago landscape architect Jens Jensen spent two days establishing a bulb planting plan for the Bathhouse Row promenade. (NPS, 1917) The main landscape development was designed and completed by Captain Robert Stevens of the Army Corps of Engineers and included many greenways and park areas which still provide a backdrop for the urban bathhouse promenade. The National Park Service is presently restating many of those landscape plans in their 1991 schedule.

Summary

George Washington Vanderbilt and Samuel Fordyce were affected greatly by their backgrounds and Victorian times. Even if their wealth allowed them the luxury of a more selfish lifestyle, their expenditures also affected their chosen hometowns. Fordyce remained largely in the wings of many of his philanthropic endeavors while Vanderbilt openly extended his holdings. Nevertheless, both of these men left legacies of unique architecture and landscape as well as the continued protection for those legacies. Modern tourism principles can be linked to the success of these two resorts. The unique architecture and the seemingly boundless landscape surrounding those structures are two important connections. Perhaps greater though is the cultural heritage that is preserved at these places. The timelessness that is contained there because of the vision, energy, and ability of these two men is a heritage all Americans can share. Successful resort developments during the Victorian Era might be measured against these sterling examples.

Author's Footnote
This summer, after completing what seemed to be the last research for this comparison, out of curiosity I visited the historic, parklike Bellfontaine Cemetery in St. Louis to see the grave of Samuel Fordyce. Located on what is commonly called "Millionaire's Row," overlooking the Mississippi River delta, the simple Fordyce marker is aligned with others of more grand and prominent scale. The cemetery reads like a *Who's Who of Fame and Fortune*; across from Fordyce's grave one mausoleum by Louis Sullivan holds National Register designation. Samuel Fordyce, in death as in life, looks simply beyond the trappings of wealth onto the rolling land and river and upon an example of the extended landscape he fought so intensely to preserve.

Bibliography

Asheville, North Carolina: The Land of the Sky. Asheville: Asheville Board of Trade, 1905.

Asheville Citizen-Times, September 11, 1932. n.p., December 13, 1936, October 21, 1962, March 26, 1950.

Auchincloss, Louis. *The Vanderbilt Era, Profiles of a Gilded Age.* New York: Charles Scribner's Sons, 1989.

Baldwin, Cathleen, Research Assistant, The Biltmore Company, submittal to author, July, 1991.

Beveridge, Charles E., and Carolyn F. Hoffman. *The Master List of Design Projects of the Olmsted Firm, 1857-1950.* Boston, MA: Massachusetts Association for Olmsted Parks, 1987.

Brower, Nancy. "Highland Happenings, Shut-In Trail," *The Asheville Times*, July 13, 1978.

Brown, Dee. *The American Spa, Hot Springs, Arkansas.* Little Rock, Arkansas: Rose Publishing Company, 1982.

Cohen, Erik. "The Impact of Tourism on the Physical Environment." *Annals of Tourism Research*, 5 (2), April/June 1978, 215-237.

Dykman, Wilma. *The French Broad.* New York: Rinehart and Co., 1955.

Fordyce, Samuel Wesley. *Autobiography.* Unpublished, 1919.

Eubank, Fanny D. "Drovers' Trail Riders Found Adventure and. Profit In Early Days," *Asheville Citizen-Times*, Asheville, North Carolina, Sunday, June 28, 1936.

Gunn, Clare A. *Tourism Planning.* New York: Taylor and Francis, 1988.

Gustavus, Myers. *The Ending of Hereditary American Fortunes.* New York: Julian Messner, 1939.

Harshaw, Lou. *Asheville, Places of Discovery.* Asheville, North Carolina, Bright Mountain Books, 1980.

Health Resorts of the South, Boston, Massachusetts: George H. Chapin, 1892.

Lynes, Russell. *The Tastemakers, The Shaping of American Popular Taste.* New York: Dover Publications, Inc., 1980.

Mann, William. "Sittin' on Jekyl, Planned by H. W. S. Cleveland, Georgia's Jekyl Island Club Was America's First 'Winter Newport,'" In *Selected Works: Council of Educators in Landscape Architecture, 1990 Conference Proceedings.* Washington, D.C.: Landscape Architecture Foundation.

National Park Service, Department of the Interior, pamphlet, "Shut-In Trail, Blue Ridge Parkway and Pisgah National Forest, A National Recreational Trail."

National Park Service, Hot Springs, Arkansas. Construction and Preservation Programs. File D-22, general, 1917-1932. Norman, Geoffrey, "Pop Hollandsworth's Secret Hiking Trail," *Esquire Magazine*, August, 1978.

Olmsted, Fredrick Law, to William A. Stiles, 10 March, 1895. Letter.

Paige, John C., and Laura Soulliere Harrison. *Out of the Vapors: A Social and Architectural History of Bathhouse Row.* U.S. Department of the Interior/National Park Service, 1987.

Pigram, John, Jr. "Environment Implications of Tourism Development," *Annals of Tourism Research*, 7(4), 1980, 554-583.

Savage, Charles C. *Architecture of the Private Streets of St. Louis, The Architects and the Houses They Designed.* Columbia, Missouri: University of Missouri Press, 1987.

Scully, Francis J., M.D. *Hot Springs Arkanasas and Hot Springs National Park. The Story of a City and the Nation's Health Resort.* Little Rock, Arkansas: Hansen Co. & Pioneer Press, 1966.

Sondley, F. S. *A History of Buncombe County, North Carolina.* Spartanburg: The Reprint Company, 1977. (Originally printed by Advocate Print of Asheville, 1930.)

Smith, Richard Sharpe, *My Sketch Book.* Asheville: Samuel J. Fisher, 1901.

Swaim, Douglas. *Cabins and Castles, The History and Architecture of Buncombe County, North Carolina.* Asheville, North Carolina: Historic Resources Commission of Asheville and Buncombe County, 1981.

Tessier, Mitzi Schaden. *Asheville, A Pictorial History.* Norfolk, Virginia: The Donning Company, 1982.

Vanderbilt, Arthur T., II. *Fortune's Children, The Fall of the House of Vanderbilt.* New York: William Morrow, 1989.

Ward, Susan. *The Gilded Age at Biltmore Estate.* Asheville, North Carolina, The Biltmore Company, 1990.

Ward, Susan M., and Michael K. Smith. *Biltmore Estate.* Asheville, North Carolina, 1989.

The Appalachian Trail Across the Cumberland Valley
A Case Study of Linear Park Design with Cultural Landscape Preservation, Agricultural Preservation, and Landscape Ecology
Neil P. Korostoff, Thomas G. Yahner, Timothy P. Johnson

INTRODUCTION

In 1921 Benton MacKaye, one of the founders of the Regional Planning Association of America, proposed an experiment in regional planning that included a greenbelt or "open way" through the Appalachian Mountains of the Eastern United States that would serve as a geographical control for urban growth from the great cities of the Atlantic coast and piedmont and a contiguous system of natural reserves for recreational activities and the development of silvicultural and agricultural resources. Though this visionary concept of the linear park as an element of regional planning, conservation, and recreational development was largely unrealized, the idea of a simple foot path from Maine to Georgia captured the imagination of a significant number of outdoor enthusiasts. Volunteer effort established the 2,000-mile Appalachian Trail and in the ensuing decades has maintained the trail, built shelters and bridges, and operated hostels.

The trail passed mainly through public lands, across state and national parks and forests, but where there was no alternative, it crossed privately owned land, or at the last resort, traveled on public roads and highways. Because the trail follows the Appalachian Mountains, and because the trail is intended as a wilderness experience, much of the footpath follows ridge tops and remote mountain terrain. In several places however, the trail must cross valleys where it intersects roads, population centers, agriculture and other land uses that contrast with the wilderness experience. In recent years, development pressure has threatened the continuity of the trail and prompted the federal government to acquire a corridor of land for the trail so that it may be preserved for future generations. The priority for land acquisition has been in those places most threatened by urban growth and development. One such place is the Cumberland Valley of Pennsylvania. The Cumberland Valley is the longest valley crossing on the Appalachian Trail, some 16 miles across, and has long been recognized as a important missing link. In 1975 the Department of Landscape Architecture at Penn State University studied the feasibility of various valley crossing alignments for the trail. Shortly thereafter the U.S. Department of the Interior, through the National Park Service (N.P.S.), began the process of acquiring land for the Appalachian Trail Conference in order to provide a corridor of public land for the trail to cross the Cumberland Valley. (Figure 1).

The corridor for the trail consists in part of a low wooded ridge, the adjacent intensively cultivated rolling valley framed by the thickly forested parallel mountain ridges of the Appalachian Range. It crosses two streams, major highways and local roads. Adjacent to the trail corridor, agricultural land is rapidly giving way to suburban development and transportation facilities. The corridor land is managed by the Cumberland Valley Appalachian Trail Management Committee (CVATMC), a local arm of the Appalachian Trail Conference. In 1988 the CVATMC sought the assistance of the Department of Landscape Architecture at the Pennsylvania State University to develop a plan for the trail and corridor which would

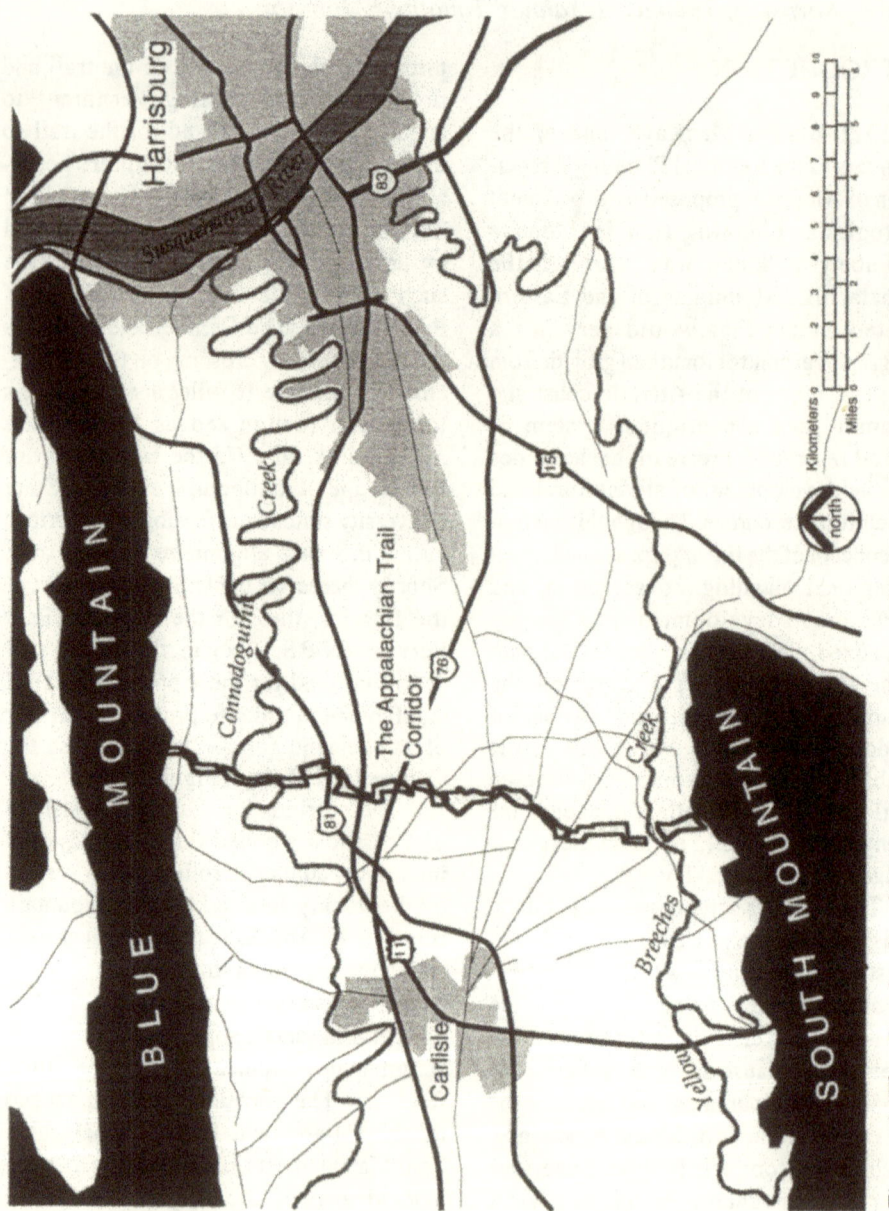

Figure 1: The Cumberland Valley Region of Pennsylvania and the Appalachian Trail Corridor

recommend an alignment for the trail, and to devise a design and management plan for the approximately 1,600 acres of corridor land. Funding for the project was provided through a grant from the Alexander Stewart, M.D. Foundation.

The study process entailed three distinct phases: 1) Analysis of existing conditions; 2) Development of a conceptual base; 3) Recommendations for specific design and management actions. The analysis included both an on-site and a regional scale study of the existing geological, ecological, visual, and cultural conditions. This information was mapped using the Macintosh Computer in the drawing software *Claris CAD*. Conclusions were drawn and summaries compiled of the ecological environments, the visual characteristics, and the cultural resources of the corridor. From this analysis, a conceptual base was developed—a detailed set of ideas, goals, objectives, and proposed methods that would inform the specific recommendations for design and management of the corridor land.

THE STEWARDSHIP CHALLENGE

Early in the process the design team realized that the acquisition of a corridor for the Appalachian Trail across the Cumberland Valley presented a new set of problems for the Appalachian Trail Conference and its local representative, the CVATMC. In its previous history trail management had for the most part been performed by just such local volunteer organizations. Their activities consisted mainly of blazing or marking the trail, removing fallen trees, building rough bridges and drainage for the footpath, maintaining shelters and other rustic trail facilities. The newly acquired corridor of some 1,600 acres of largely agricultural land constituted an unprecedented management challenge for this small group of volunteers, trail enthusiasts, and their small paid staff. The most basic decisions regarding trail alignment, access, and corridor land management required an examination of fundamental stewardship values, goals, and objectives on the part of the ATC and the CVATMC. The full range of corridor design and management issues, and the importance of the corridor for the Appalachian Trail and the Cumberland Valley region, were considered together under the title of "stewardship" issues.

When contrasted with the totality of the Appalachian Trail, the new corridor offered many new and unique conditions. For most of its 2,000-mile length the Trail largely traverses forested areas on the crest of the Appalachian Mountains remote from urban development and the modern world. The Cumberland Valley is an intensively cultivated region, crossed and recrossed by major highways, and serving as the recent locus of suburban growth from the nearby cities of Harrisburg and Carlisle, Pennsylvania. Through-hikers, those Maine to Georgia stalwarts, and other long distance recreational backpackers, would encounter a valley landscape very different from the mountain vistas common to most of the Trail. What attitude should the new corridor and trail take toward these new landscapes?

Not only is the Cumberland Valley physiographically distinct from the Appalachian ridges, but in many respects its ecology is profoundly different. The underlying limestone and shale geology has weathered and eroded to create a rolling valley floor, where surface water is rare, but groundwater abundant in soluble, cavernous limestone bedrock. The basic, nutrient rich soils derived from these substrata, in this humid, temperate environment, give rise to a community of plants and animals distinctly different from that on Appalachian ridges. While most of the forests of basswood, hickory, oak, ash, and hackberry native to this soil have been removed for agriculture, what role shall the unique natural history of this valley have in the management of the trail and corridor landscapes? And what of particularly sensitive natural resources of the corridor—springs, wetlands, and rare or endangered species? How shall they figure in the ATC's plans for the Cumberland Valley corridor?

The ecological value of the corridor has important implications for the entire Cumberland Valley region. The preservation of biological diversity has become an important conservation issue. The diverse mosaic of locally adapted deciduous forest biotic communities which once covered the valley variously cut, cleared, burned and grazed through the past three hundred years for agriculture, urban development, industrial, and commercial use. While some of the forest cover has regenerated over time, the resultant landscape, especially that of the Cumberland Valley, is a patchwork of farm fields, wood lots, hedgerows, and residential and commercial areas, all divided, or connected, by narrow corridors of utility rights-of-way, highways, etc. Conditions such as these, technically described as habitat fragmentation, separate populations of native wildlife and plants into units too small to sustain genetic viability resulting in a loss of biological diversity. In rapidly urbanizing areas habitat fragmentation is accelerated as large estates, farms, and even abandoned former agricultural land is subdivided for residential and commercial use. In light of these important regional ecological issues how should this marvelous new potentially connective linear park be designed and managed?

The landscapes of the Cumberland Valley also contain well preserved and illustrative examples of its three hundred year European history which, sadly, are threatened and rapidly disappearing under the rising tide of suburban sprawl. Houses, barns, farm steads, cemeteries, roads, walls, fences—what approach shall the ATC take toward these cultural resources? Are they worthy of the hikers' attention or potential liabilities and maintenance headaches? While the corridor itself contains several structures of historic significance, many others were visible from corridor lands. Can these views be considered in trail design? And what of the biotic cultural resources-the hedgerows, orchards, field patterns and resting trees-how shall the ATC, as management steward for the land, approach these objects of living, perishable history? While agriculture is still a dominant land use in the Cumberland Valley, it is rapidly being supplanted by urbanization and transportation related activities. Much of the corridor land is excellently suited for farming and was formerly in agricultural use. As farming diminishes in the valley, what role should the corridor lands play in that land use change? Is the agricultural history of the Cumberland Valley a worthy subject for the attention of the through hiker as well?

While the Appalachian Trail is first and foremost a hiking facility the acquisition of this important corridor presses the questions of the role of this new linear park in the land use and recreational open space issues of the region. Is the new corridor a regional green belt, a bar to urbanization and suburban sprawl? Will future residential subdivisions crowd its boundaries to benefit from the open space amenity it provides? Is the Appalachian Trail primarily for long-distance backpackers, a kind of limited access hiking path, or shall it also be available for short-term day use by local residents? Shall its design and management be integrated with that of local parks and open spaces? It was imperative that these and many other questions be asked and answered as design and planning of the corridor began.

THE CONCEPTUAL BASE

Once the corridor land and the region were inventoried and analyzed, the Challenges facing the ATC were articulated, and specific questions were asked, it was then necessary to mold a vision of the trail corridor that would integrate the Trail with the Cumberland Valley landscape. This conceptual base would be a set of ideas, concepts, or principles from which specific design and management recommendations could be made. Without this base the corridor plan would simply be a loose group of reactions and responses without integrity or purpose.

The concepts were seen as falling into two basic areas—those relating to land stewardship and those relating to the experience of hiking the trail. Land stewardship included three areas—the cultural, the ecological, and the agricultural stewardship of the landscape. Hiking experience addresses the relationship between the hiker and the landscape.

CULTURAL STEWARDSHIP — The cultural artifacts that exist within the trail corridor should be retained and incorporated into the design in a way that allows for their preservation.

It is assumed that the land-use change underway in the Cumberland Valley will eventually convert much of the agrarian landscape to residential and commercial uses, and so doing, erase or mask most of the artifacts that comprise this distinctive landscape character. However, the ownership of the trail corridor by the National Park Service ensures that this land will be preserved in perpetuity and presents the opportunity for any cultural resources retained within the corridor to also be preserved, even if the cultural landscape is lost elsewhere in the valley.

Both the biotic and the structural cultural resources within the Trail corridor should be retained and preserved as historical artifacts that, when experienced in the total context of the trail corridor, serve to complete a picture of the human interaction with the landscape. The artifacts of the vernacular cultural and historic landscape that exist within the trail corridor should be incorporated into the trail design in a way that allows them to be part of an integrated landscape rather than become a collection of separate and unrelated pieces. The greatest number of these historic landscape elements should be retained and they should remain within their natural relationships. These relationships might include house, barn, and fields; stone wall, hedgerow, and pasture; or a cemetery in a field within sight of 200-year-old houses.

Biotic Cultural Resources are defined here as those communities of plants and animals that were associated with the agrarian landscape of the Cumberland Valley prior to the recent conversion from an agricultural to a residential land use. These communities may include hedgerows, fields, pastures, gardens, and ponds. The biotic cultural resources within the trail corridor should be retained and preserved as historical artifacts that, when experienced in the total context of the trail corridor, serve to complete a picture of the human interaction with the landscape.

- Remaining examples of the historic small field and hedgerow pattern that exists within the corridor should be retained as open space surrounded by hedgerows. These fields should either be maintained in cultivation, put into pasture, or managed as permanent meadow.

- Old hedgerows should be retained.

- Resting trees, that were left standing alone in fields by the early farmers as a shady place to rest horses, should be retained, and if possible, the trail should be routed to pass by them.

- Gardens, fruit trees, and domestic trees and shrubs should be retained where they occur around farm steads.
- Ponds within the trail corridor should be retained.

Structural Cultural Resources may be defined as the constructed features in the landscape that relate to the agricultural period prior to the conversion of the land use from agricultural to residential. This includes such features as houses, barns, cemeteries, fences, and stone walls. The structural resources within the trail corridor should be retained and preserved as historical artifacts that, taken together, provide clues to the cultural history of the corridor and the entire valley.

- Stone walls should be retained, should be kept free of vegetation, and should not be broken at trail crossings.
- Where stone walls have been broken, they should be restored if the same quality of workmanship can be attained to match the remaining portion of the wall.
- Houses and barns and outbuildings within the corridor that are of historic value and in restorable condition should be retained. The buildings should be stabilized, their exteriors restored, and interiors renovated to meet the functional requirements of an adaptive reuse.
- If it is not possible to retain a house or barn, the structure should be carefully demolished to retain the stone foundation, and any walkways, trees, or garden sites associated with the farm stead should also be preserved.
- Cemeteries should be restored and maintained so that their features are intact and protected from deterioration.
- Deteriorated remnants of five-rail, split rail fences should be measured and documented so that this form may be used in the future where small amounts of fencing are needed.

ECOLOGICAL STEWARDSHIP—The ecological components of the corridor should be preserved, restored, or enhanced so that the greatest diversity of habitats within the corridor are allowed to function as part of broader ecological systems.

Analysis of the trail corridor and the adjacent land concluded that:

- the corridor landscape is ecologically diverse but fragmented into small habitat patches by the agricultural and other land uses;
- the few remaining forested areas are small and have a disproportionately large amount of edge and little shaded interior;
- access to water is limited for many species;
- the movement of plants and animals is barred by large areas of agricultural land transportation corridors and other land uses;
- the rapid conversion of the adjacent land from an agricultural to a residential use may further reduce connections for the movement of plants and animals by eliminating hedgerows and wood lots adjacent to the corridor and reducing the areas of native habitats within the valley.

Therefore, the corridor design should enhance the diversity of native habitats, establish forested corridors, and open free access to water resources. The concepts address those goals by looking at issues of preservation, reforestation and restoration, and connections.

Preservation—Maintain and protect all existing physical and native biological components of the natural environment, including the natural vegetation, wildlife, soil and water resources within the trail corridor.

- Areas of native vegetation, mature forests, and mature individual trees should be preserved and protected.
- Fields that are released from agriculture should be managed to return to native vegetation. Some areas should be managed to remain at an early stage of succession, while others will be allowed to succeed to forest.
- All water resources including springs, wetlands, ponds, and streams should be preserved and surrounded with a one hundred foot wide buffer of native vegetation.

Reforestation and Restoration—Patches of native valley forest types, hedgerows, and successional habitats, such as permanent meadows and old-fields, should be re-established within the trail corridor.

- Forest patches should be reestablished with the greatest possible area and a minimum width of three hundred feet, as a means to establish forest interior habitat.
- Reforestation should be done with forest species native to the limestone valley, and all efforts should be made to ascertain specific locations for specific forest types within the valley. Wherever possible local genotypes should be propagated for reforestation.
- Exotic and invasive species must not be introduced and where possible, management efforts should aim for the elimination of nonnative pest species such as multiflora rose, Japanese barberry, and Oriental bittersweet.
- A buffer of natural vegetation, preferably forest, of at least one hundred feet in width should be established

around water resources and wetlands to protect wetlands from disturbance, to filter fertilizer and pesticide residue from agricultural or urban runoff, to enhance the ecologic and habitat value of wetlands, and to increase the access for wildlife to water.

Connections—Wherever possible a continuous forested strip of three hundred feet minimum width should be established within the trail corridor to connect both existing and reforested patches of valley forest. Connections should be made between forested patches within the corridor and to forested patches outside the trail corridor.

- If possible, patches of valley forest should be established wherever the corridor joins a patch of existing valley forest adjacent to the corridor.
- A continuous forested strip connecting forest patches within the corridor should be established at the greatest possible width, while meeting the agricultural and open space requirements of the hiking experience. This strip should have a minimum width of three hundred feet.
- A forested strip should be established to connect water resources and wetlands to forested patches and other habitats.

AGRICULTURAL STEWARDSHIP— The prime farmland that has been in continuous agricultural use for greater than 200 years should be incorporated into the corridor design and agriculture Should be allowed to continue as a viable land use in a changing landscape.

Active agriculture should be incorporated into the trail corridor, partly as a cultural/historical feature, and partly as a component of the contemporary landscape. With agricultural land rapidly disappearing from the adjacent landscape, retention of farms in the trail corridor will enhance local landscape diversity as well as local cultural diversity.

Incorporating agriculture into the trail corridor presents several challenges. First, farming practices must be managed to minimize soil loss and to protect water resources. Field design should follow best agricultural conservation practices including crop rotation, strip cropping, and grass waterways. Pest management should be carried out with a minimum of pesticides and herbicides within a program of Integrated Pest Management, as prescribed by the National Park Service.

Second, agricultural fields should be designed so that they can be farmed using contemporary machinery and practices. However in the event of a conflict between agricultural efficiency and the considerations of trail design, or the conservation of cultural or ecological resources, it is agricultural efficiency that should be compromised rather than the other values. Conflicts could be resolved by subsidizing the agricultural activities or by taking specific fields out of agricultural production and allowing them to become permanent meadows managed as a substitute cover.

Third, agricultural fields must be compatible with the trail so that the sometimes conflicting requirement of each can be incorporated into a unified design that minimizes interference of one use with the other. In all cases the overall requirements of the trail should be the leading consideration in the overall design. The direction of cultivation should follow the direction of the trail and the trail should not cut across the direction of cultivation. The trail may be incorporated into the field design by running between contour strips but should be given a sufficient right of way to allow for the various types of machinery to work and turn without ever crossing the actual footpath. Where the trail must cross a pasture, it should be fenced to eliminate the possibility of confrontation between hikers and grazing animals.

THE HIKING EXPERIENCE—**In recognition of the important role that this corridor would play in recreational open-space for the changing Cumberland Valley Region the trail should be designed so that it is accessible, usable and interesting for repeated day-use as well as for use by through-hikers. The experience of hiking the trail corridor in the Cumberland Valley should be designed so that: the path is spatially clear; the experience is aesthetically and visually interesting; and the experience of hiking the trail is educational revealing the history of the Cumberland Valley, the ecological, and the geological environment to the hiker.**

When walking the trail, the overall design of the trail corridor should lead the hiker through the landscape with minimal reliance on signage and trail markers. The hiker should not be unintentionally lead off the trail by confusing spatial messages. When the trail corridor was purchased by the National Park Service, the corridor boundary did not always coincide with existing landscape Alights. In many cases the boundary ran through the middle of an existing field so that there was no clear definition to the corridor. In such cases corridor design should redefine the corridor edge and reestablish spatial units within the corridor. The design of the immediate trail environment should help to guide the hiker along the footpath and through the valley. Various devises could be used to orient the hiker such as directing the trail toward distant focal points, aligning the trail along existing linear features like hedgerows and streams, and utilizing the topography as a source of direction and movement.

In order to create interest and provide a varied experience of the landscape, the trail should pass through or adjacent to a diversity of spatial situations. Throughout the trail corridor the hiker should walk through a series of "rooms" of different sizes, scales, and characters each the result of a different type and maturity of plant community interacting with topography. The trail should interact with different spaces from a variety of vantage points—from the center, from the edge, or from the outside looking in. The trail should relate to the topography in a variety of ways to create interest and to reveal the landform Likewise the trail should relate the great diversity of individual cultural, ecological, and geological features within the corridor. Some features are individual points, while others are linear. Point features include old trees, rock outcrops, springs, ponds, and buildings. Linear features include streams, stone walls, hedgerows, and abandoned roads. To create interest while revealing the features in the landscape, the trail should interact with these features but relate to them in a variety of ways.

The various components of the landscape—the topography, spaces, and the many individual features—can each be seen as layers of experience that flow through the trail corridor. Within each layer, the specific pieces fit together to create a sequence of experiences that reveals the landscape as fully as possible while creating variety in the way that the landscape is experienced. On the ground, these layers will fit together much like the harmonic lines of a musical score—each one working well in its own right, but combining to create a total composition.

PROJECT EXAMPLE

One illustration of how these concepts were applied to the site is at the southern side of the valley where the trail meets South Mountain. Here, the agricultural fields were without contour strips and without hedgerows. There was no forest connection through the corridor between South Mountain on one end of this section and the Yellow Breeches Creek on the other. And no opportunity existed for a trail route through the farm land. The recommendations called for a three-hundred-foot strip to be reforested as a connection for the movement of plants and animals between these two environments. It was recommended that the agricultural land be laid out in contour strips. The trail was designed to be between forest and agriculture, in places within the forest, and to also run between contour strips with agriculture on both sides. The layout of the Agricultural strips was intended to be visually appealing to the hiker, to maximize soil conservation, and to be able to be farmed profitably. The following set of recommendations for one section of the Trail corridor is an example of the management and design recommendations provided to the A.T.C. It is keyed to the accompanying map (Figure 2).

Section 2

In this section, the Sunday property (Figure 3) is an entire farm of good quality but eroded agricultural land. The nineteenth-century farmhouse establishes a focus for the farm and presents an opportunity for adaptive reuse of the structure. Wide open views are available to South Mountain, as well as to potentially developable land to the east and west. The forest and wildlife connection between the valley bottom and the adjacent upland is severed. An important concept is to establish this forest connection between South Mountain and the floodplain forest of the Yellow Breeches Creek, as a functional linkage for people, plants, and wildlife.

2 A. Hedgerow—A hedgerow should

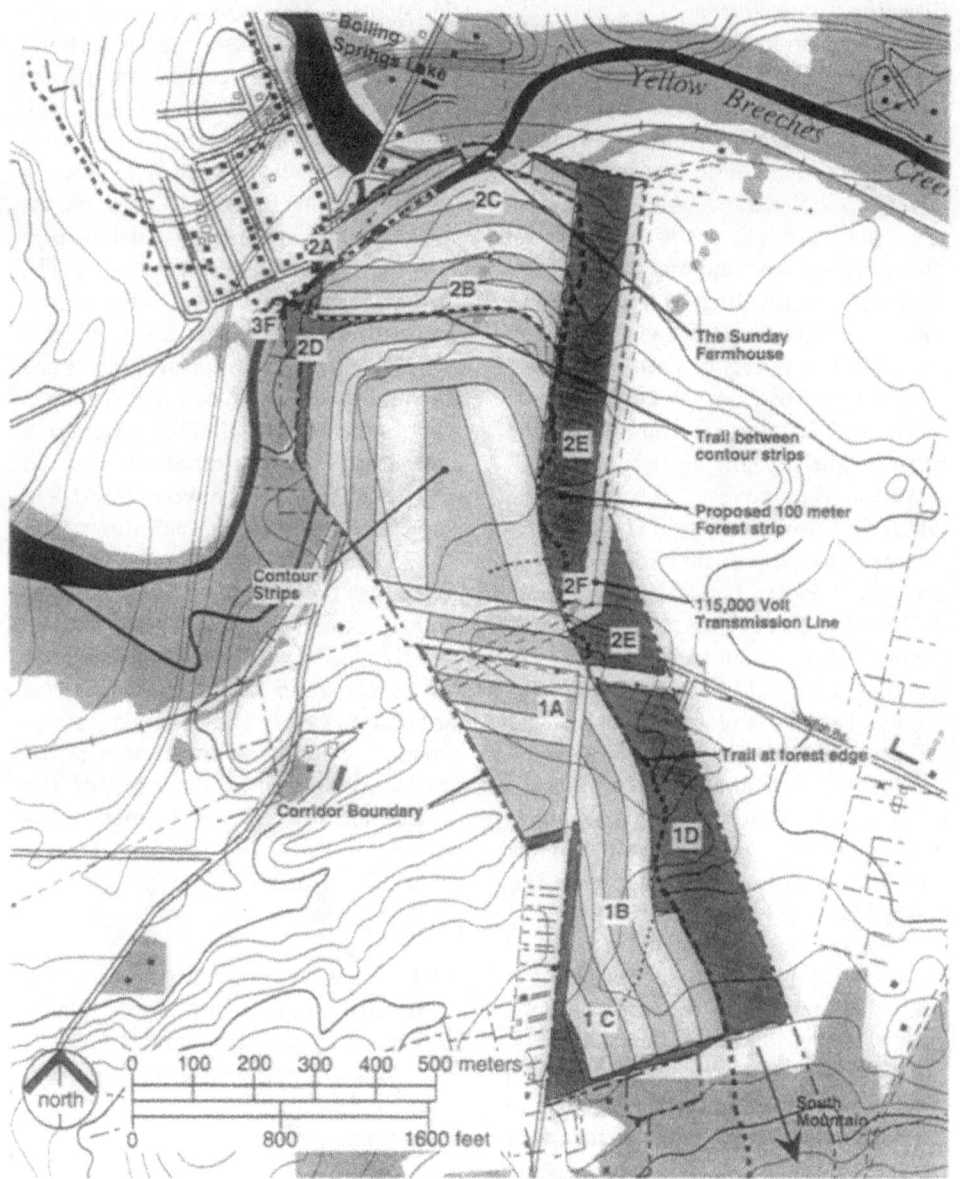

Figure 2. Sections 2 and 1 of the Recommendations for the Appalachian Trail Corridor.

be planted to screen the view from this section to the pallet factory at the northwest corner and to the pallet stacks along the northern boundary of the corridor.

2 B. Agricultural Practices and Trail Alignment—This section should remain in agriculture, using contour strips and grass waterways to minimize soil loss, according to the recommendations of the SCS. The Trail should pass between strips, following the undulating topography as the strips wind through the landscape. The trail will pass an existing cluster of trees orienting hikers traveling in either direction and the hiker will be able to see the lowland forest along the Yellow Breeches Creek.

2 C. Hostel / Alternate Route / Side Trail—The limestone Sunday farmhouse should remain, be restored and used, if possible, as a hostel. This four-opening, two-front-door house faces the railroad. It seems possible that, when the house was built in the mid nineteenth century, it faced a road that was later replaced by the railroad. The barn is missing but a kitchen garden site, a planting of lilacs, the site of a privy, and the site of a clothes line remain and could become the basis of a domestic landscape restoration. An alternate route for the Trail should be created, bringing the Trail to the house.

2 D. Screen—This area should be allowed to return to forest to screen the view to the pallet plant and the adjacent houses. This wooded area will also limit unauthorized vehicular access to the corridor.

2 E. Forest Connection—A three-hundred-foot wide band of forest should be established as a connection for the movement of plants and animals between the Yellow Breeches Creek and South Mountain. Native species should be established with seeds, seedlings or trees and removal of exotic species.

2 F. Power Line—This 115,000 volt transmission line has an easement of one hundred and twenty feet. The area within this easement should be maintained as a woody old-field or perennial meadow.

Section 1

This section has good quality agricultural soil that is eroded in some places. Open views are available throughout the section to existing development and land with development potential. The present agricultural pattern conflicts with the direc-

Figure 3. The Sunday Farmhouse offers the opportunity for reuse as a hostel.

tional needs of the Trail as well as with accepted soil conservation practices. This section lacks the forest connection to Yellow Breeches Creek.

1 A. Safe Road Crossing—The Trail should cross Leidigh Road at its intersection with Gutshall Road.

1 B. Agricultural Practices—This section should remain in agriculture, using contour strips and grass waterways to minimize soil loss, according to the recommendations of the SCS. The fields should run in a north/south direction so that they follow the directional requirements of the trail.

1 C. Hedgerow—A fifty-foot hedgerow containing some native evergreens should be planted along the western edge of the corridor as a screen. Some openings should remain to provide filtered views to the houses along Gutshall Road associated with the iron mining on South Mountain in the nineteenth century.

1 D. Forest Connection—A three-hundred-foot-wide band of forest should be established along the east side of the corridor as a connection for the movement of plants and animals between the Yellow Breeches Creek and South Mountain. The Trail should pass along the western edge of the proposed forest corridor. In the short distance between the top of South Mountain and the Yellow Breeches Creek, the hiker will move through a series of plant communities including those of the ridge top and mountain slope, the moist lower slope communities, the valley and floodplain forest communities.

ACKNOWLEDGMENTS

This study was undertaken in cooperation with the Cumberland Valley Appalachian Trail Management Committee, the Appalachian Trail Conference, and the National Park Service. Funding for the project was provided through a grant from the Alexander Stewart, M.D. Foundation. The original study performed by the Department of Landscape Architecture at Penn State University. The project team, headed by Professor A. Mark Battaglia, included Associate Professor Daniel Jones, and the authors, as principal investigators. Bonj Sczcygiel contributed to the sections on trail philosophy and the history of the Cumberland Valley.

BIBLIOGRAPHY

Baker, Joseph. "A Cultural Resource Assessment of the Cumberland Valley Trail Relocation for the Appalachian National Scenic Trail". (Unpublished manuscript. Harrisburg, PA; August 1989).

Becher, Albert E., and Samuel I. Root. *Groundwater and Geology of The Cumberland Valley, Cumberland County, Pennsylvania* (Harrisburg, PA; Pennsylvania Geological Survey; 1981).

Beers, Frederick W. *Atlas of Cumberland County* (New York; F. W. Beers and Company; 1872).

Birchard, William, Jr., and Robert D. Proudman. *Trail Design, Construction, and Maintenance* (Harpers Ferry, WV; The Appalachian Trail Conference; 1981).

Burch, William R., Jr., Editor. *Long Distance Trails: The Appalachian Trail as a Guide to Future Research and Management Needs* (New Haven, CT; Yale University; 1979).

Burgess, Robert L., and David M. Sharpe, Editors. *Forest Island Dynamics in Man-dominated Landscapes* (New York; Springer-Verlag; 1981).

Flippo, Herbert N., Jr. *Springs of Pennsylvania* (Harrisburg, PA; Commonwealth of Pennsylvania, Department of Environmental Resources, Office of Resources Management; 1974).

Forman, Richard T. T., and Michel Godron. *Landscape Ecology* (New York; John Wiley and Sons, Inc.; 1986).

Foster, Charles H. W. *The Appalachian National Scenic Trail.: A Time To Be Bold.* (Charles H. W. Foster, Needham, MA, 1987).

Glass, Joseph W. *The Pennsylvania Culture Region, A View From the Barn.* (Ann Arbor, MI; UMI Research Press, 1986).

Harris, Larry D. *The Fragmented Forest: Island Biogeography Theory and the Preservation of Biotic Diversity* (Chicago, IL; University of Chicago Press; 1984).

Hunter, Malcolm L., Jr. *Wildlife Forests and Forestry: Principles of Managing Forests for Biological Diversity* (Englewood Cliffs, NJ; Prentice-Hall, Inc.; 1990).

Johnson, Hugh. "The Appalachian Trail and Beyond." *Journal of American Institute of Architects* (October 1971): 23-27.

Lewis, Pierce. "Defining a Sense of Place" *The Southern Quarterly* (Spring-Summer 1979) 24-46

Little, Charles E. *Greenways for America* (Baltimore and London; The Johns Hopkins University Press; 1990).

MacKaye, Benton. "An Appalachian Trail: A Project in Regional Planning." *The Journal of the American Institute Of Architects* (1921).

MacKaye, Benton. "The Appalachian Trail: A Guide to the Study of Nature." *Scientific Monthly* (April 1932): 330-342.

MacKaye, Benton. "Wilderness Ways." *Landscape Architecture* 19 (July 1929): 237-249.

National Park Service, *National Trails Assessment* (Washington, DC; U.S. Department of Interior; 1986).

The Atlas of Pennsylvania. A cooperative project of the three commonwealth research universities; Temple University, eds. Cuff, David, William Young; University of Pennsylvania, ed. Edward Muller; The Pennsylvania State University, eds. Wilbur Zelinsky, Ronald. (Philadelphia; Temple University Press; 1989).

Proudman, Robert D., and Reuben Rajala. *AMC Field Guide to Trail Building and Maintenance 2nd Edition* (Boston, MA; The Appalachian Mountain Club; 1981).

Wilshusen, J. Peter. *Geology of the Appalachian Trail in Pennsylvania* (Harrisburg, PA; Pennsylvania Geological Survey; 1983).

Zelinsky, Wilbur. "The Pennsylvania Town: An Overdue Geographical Account" *The Geographical Review* (April 1977) 127-147.

A Visual Assessment of the New River

Wayne E. Williams, Delmar W. Barchert, Paul L. Gaskill, and Holly Pierce

INTRODUCTION

The New River is the second-oldest river in the world, and only the mighty Nile is thought to be older. In 1976, a 26.5-mile corridor received protection from both the State of North Carolina and the federal government. The purpose of the North Carolina Natural and Scenic Rivers Act of 1971 is: "To protect rivers with outstanding natural, scenic, educational, geological, recreational, historic, fish and wildlife, scientific, and cultural values." The federal National Wild and Scenic Rivers Act provides for a scenic river to be: "Free of impoundments, with shorelines or watersheds still largely primitive and shorelines largely undeveloped, but accessible in places by roads."

The designation of the New River corridor as a scenic river brought a collective sigh of relief to those who had fought a 14-year battle to keep the Appalachian Power Company from building a hydroelectric power generating dam on the river. The battle is detailed in Schoenbaum's (1979) *The New River Controversy*.

The protection provided by the designation is detailed in the statutes:

> The Natural and Scenic Rivers Act offers protection for designated river segments by restricting project works—such as dams, reservoirs, water conduits, transmission lines, and water resources projects that would have direct and adverse affects—(G.S. 113A-44); by permitting acquisition of riparian lands in either fee simple or lesser interests, such as conservation easements (G.S. 113A-38); and by management activities that may be instituted by the Department of Natural Resources and Community Development in performing its duties and responsibilities (G.S. 113A-36).
>
> Of three types of protection authorized by the Natural and Scenic Rivers Act, only the restriction on project works automatically occurs upon designation. Riparian lands are not affected until acquisition of land or interests in land takes place by the state. For land acquisition (other than by donation), development and operations to take place, legislative appropriations are necessary. (State of North Carolina, 1990, p. 3)

Federal and state designations, however, have failed to truly protect the New River scenic corridor as it meanders through Ashe and Allegheny Counties of Western North Carolina. The failure is a result of the lack of acquisition funds from the legislature.

There has been ample cause for concern expressed in the print media. Thompson (1990) alarmed the public by reporting in *The Mountain Times*: "Officials in the National Park Service have discussed decommissioning the New River." The National Rivers Coalition listed the New River as one of the *ten most endangered rivers* in America for 1990. The endangered status has been announced in such publications as *Trilogy, Canoe Magazine*, and various newspapers. A team of state officials examined the river corridor in 1989. Collins, a member of the group, stated that the river corridor:

> is seriously threatened by uncontrolled growth and destructive development within the visual corridor. There are large subdivisions planned and under development throughout much of the 26-mile corridor. They are clear cutting on near vertical slopes and building substandard roads creating severe

erosion problems and severe adverse impacts on the visual corridor. (Thompson, p. 1)

Further evidence of threats to the River is provided by Albee (1988), author of *The South Fork New River Survey Study—Draft Report*. He concludes:

> We know substandard development is occurring, that more will occur in the near future, and that there is relatively little environmental degradation which we can show to underline the urgent need for further regulation. Without some form of regulatory development, the scenic resource which North Carolina agreed to protect in taking responsibility for administration of the New River under the NWSR as amended could be legally and irreparably degraded over the course of the next few years. (Albee, p. 21)

A need existed to be able to freeze the New River in time. A visual baseline was needed against which the future scenic qualities of the corridor could be measured. A chronicle of the rapidly changing land-use patterns of the river corridor will be invaluable to future planners and researchers. Discussions were held with F. Boetler of the North Carolina Division of State Parks; Jay Wild, Superintendent of the Mt. Jefferson–New River State Park; and Paul Wetzel of the National Committee for the New River. It was determined that there was indeed a need to do a visual assessment of the New River corridor.

Support for the project was first procured from the National Rivers Coalition. The coalition is comprises several national conservation organizations: American Rivers, National Audubon Society, Sierra Club, National Association of State River Conservation Programs, American Canoe Association, American Whitewater Affiliation, National Wildlife Federation, and the Wilderness Society. The coalition makes, distributes, and monitors seed grants from Recreational Equipment, Inc. (REI). The coalition considers applications that focus on the following five criteria:

1. adds rivers for study or designation in the National Wild and Scenic Rivers System or improves the management of designated rivers;

2. improves state river programs through efforts on legislation, regulations, and/or implementation of a statewide rivers assessment;

3. promotes the passage of state or federal legislation that would facilitate federal, state, or local river protection;

4. supports increased funding for the National Park Service's Conservation Assistance Program for Fiscal Year 1991; and

5. protects and enhances natural resources and recreation for rivers subject to hydropower licensing and relicensing.

Holly Pierce, a Leisure Studies major at Appalachian State University, prepared the initial proposal to the coalition. She received technical assistance from Drs. Wayne Williams, Del Bachert, and Melissa Barth. The proposal was approved and the seed grant totaled $500. It was restricted in that it could not be used to pay salaries. The seed grant was awarded to the National Committee for the New River, the grassroots organization responsible for administrating the funds.

Additional support was secured through the Appalachian State University Environmental Issues Committee. The committee presents the annual Think Globally, Act Locally Environmental Research Service Award. The funds are available for faculty and student projects of benefit to the environment on a competitive basis. The amount of the award was $385.

METHODOLOGY

The methodology employed was relatively simple. Two-person teams traveled approximately five miles per day by canoe and prepared a videotape and photographic record of the river corridor. Videotaping was done with a hand-held Panasonic VHS Reporter camera using 3M T120 Professional Videocassettes in the 120-minute length. The team stopped approximately every half mile to take 35mm slides. Photography was made with a Nikon FM 35mm camera with a Nikor 50mm (normal) lens using Fujichrome 100 ASA film for color slides. The 50mm lens was chosen to minimize distortion of landscapes. Equipment was transported in a waterproof King Pelican case. Seven days were spent completing the survey.

STUDY REGION

The section of the river to be surveyed consisted of the 26.5 miles of the South Fork of the New River and the New River designated under the federal Wild and Scenic River System as a scenic river. This section begins approximately one mile upriver from the Wagoner Road State Park Access and ends at the North Carolina–Virginia state line. It includes four elements of the New River State Park, several commercial campgrounds, canoe rental businesses, and numerous private residences.

Photographic Survey

Preparations for the survey were begun by purchasing topographic maps corresponding to the path of the river through Ashe and Allegheny Counties. The study region included three quadrangles: Jefferson, North Carolina; Laurel Springs, North Carolina; and Mouth of Wilson, North Carolina–Virginia. Locations for photography were chosen on the basis of identifiable cultural landmarks (bridges, parks, buildings) and geological formations (streams, islands, bluffs, etc.) as indicated on the topographic maps and numbered consecutively. Landmarks were chosen to facilitate replication of the study in the future.

At each location, views of the river were recorded from the following directions: upriver, downriver, river right, and river left. Three exposures were made for each angle for a total of twelve exposures for each location to produce three complete sets of slides and videotape. In all, 49 locations were photographed for each of the four angles for a total of 196 slides for each set prepared.

Videotape Survey

Videotaping started with an audio announcement by the camera operator of the numbered position corresponding to the section of the river to be videotaped. The location was again announced each time the team stopped to take slides. When photographing was completed at each location, the opportunity was taken to resume videotaping with an upriver view. Camera operators were instructed to pan both sides of the river as well as tape directly downriver. In all, the team produced approximately eight hours of videotape.

RESEARCH APPLICATIONS

The visual assessment can be utilized in several research applications. These include a basis for future historical studies, land-use analysis, longitudinal studies, and attitudinal studies.

Historical Studies

Historical researchers are often faced with the problem of consolidating pieces of data. The task is difficult enough when dealing with printed or written documents. It is compounded when nonprint records are sought. Historical photos are often in poor condition or unlabeled. Many photographic records are the result of chance, providing only anecdotal information.

The combination of 35mm slides and videotape in a survey alleviates these problems. By sampling a large section of a linear park, researchers can prepare an extensive record of the visual nature of the resource. This type of record goes beyond the usual historical photographs of tourist attractions, family gatherings and building dedications.

Further, this study was designed to capture the river recreator's eye view of the river corridor. Both the slide and videotape records were prepared from a canoeist's vantage point. The videotape adds a constant view of the river plus an audio record of the sounds of recreation and wildlife mixed with vehicle noise, agricultural machinery, and construction equipment noise. The result should be a fascinating, extensive look into the past for historians, planners, and resource managers of the future.

Land-Use Analysis

One traditional, time-tested approach to land-use surveying is the "windshield inspection" (Goodman, 1968). Surveys of this type are routinely done from vehicles or on foot in highly developed areas such as central business districts. In order to organize the data collected through this type of survey, a land-use classification system is used. In most cases, categories of land use correspond to those used in zoning ordinances. More specific categories can be created for predominantly rural or industrial areas.

The videotape record of the New River constitutes a windshield survey from the canoeist's perspective. In conjunction with the topographic maps showing the photographic locations for the survey and county plat maps, the videotape can be used to produce a land-use map. It should be noted that the map thus created would represent only those land uses visible from the river.

While a large portion of the sample is still in open space and agriculture, a significant share reflects residential use, commercial development, and construction (see Figure 1).

Longitudinal Studies

It is hoped that available funding will enable the survey team to replicate the survey on a five-year basis. General aesthetic changes can be charted through updates of the videotape survey. A more quantitative analysis can be accomplished through replication of the slide sample. The baseline data collected through this project will provide the basis for ongoing analysis of the visual character and land use of this section of the river.

Attitudinal Studies

Reactions of sample groups to slides selected from the survey collection could form the basis for attitudinal studies. In

Figure 1.
Results of Land-Use Analysis

Land Use	Frequency	% *
Open Space	119	60
Agriculture	16	8
Residence	28	14
Commercial	5	3
Park	4	2
Road/Bridge	12	6
Development/Clearing	2	1
Utilities	2	1
Residence Under Construction	4	2
Historic Site	1	1
Residence/Agriculture	3	2
	196	100

* Rounded to the nearest whole percent

an effort to provide quantitative measures of aesthetic preferences for management approaches on U.S. Forest Service lands, Daniel and Boster (1976) developed an approach known as the Scenic Beauty Estimation Method. The approach has been shown to be both reliable and valid in measuring attitudes of identifiable groups toward landscape aesthetics.

An adaptation of the Scenic Beauty Estimation Method could be used to measure differences in perceptions of groups currently sharing the New River corridor. Organizations representing real estate developers, Christmas tree farmers, and other agricultural interests, conservation and preservation interests, and business dependent upon the river (canoe rentals, campgrounds, etc.) could be asked to rate the aesthetic value of slides from the survey collection. Further funding will be sought to support this effort.

MANAGEMENT APPLICATIONS

From a management perspective, there are several ways this study can be utilized. The basic justification for the project is predicated on the unwillingness or inability of the state government to purchase property in the scenic river corridor or to effectively control private land owner activity. Thus, publicizing the fact that this research is even necessary becomes an effective marketing application of this project.

The commitment of corporate grant funds through REI and the extensive interagency cooperation necessary to accomplish the project are further marketing attributes. Many scenic river systems are experiencing similar problems to the New River, and perhaps the study's purpose, methodology, and administration will be applicable to river corridors in other geographic locations.

As noted, the visual database created as a product of this study can serve as a basis for further historical, longitudinal, or attitudinal research. Its immediate power, however, lies in the potential impacts that visual images of river development have on the viewer. The written word, no matter how graphic, cannot convey the effects of river corridor development as can a visually explicit medium.

Given this potential, excerpts of the visual assessment project can be very useful in educating the general public about the deteriorating condition of the New River. Plans are under way to produce a 20-minute video presentation composed of tape and slides from the survey highlighting development and land-use issues. Nonprofit organizations such as the National Committee for the New River should systematically sponsor public forums designed to both update citizens and to develop a renewed interest in the preservation of the river. It was a grassroots movement that provided the impetus for initial designation of the New River into Scenic River status, and it must be a similar effort that will convince political decision makers that it is again time to act on behalf of the river.

Further presentations made to land conservancy groups or potential corporate sponsors could garner additional river support. In essence, the visual assessment project provides an excellent database for grant proposals to a variety of agencies. Especially applicable may be corporate foundations that would be willing to provide the sponsoring nonprofit agency land acquisition or scenic easement funding.

Ultimately, it is the responsibility of the North Carolina government to act on its promise to purchase and protect the land adjacent to the scenic New River corridor. This research documents the result of inactivity, but also graphically shows lengthy regions of undisturbed natural beauty that must be systematically purchased and preserved. If this visual message is carried by representatives of nonprofit organizations and concerned citizens groups, budget officers, and legislators are more likely to introduce and support funding initiatives for future river corridor preservation.

This research has visually documented the condition of the entire 26.5-mile scenic New River corridor. Copies of the photographic and video materials resulting from the study will be housed in both Appalachian State University's Appalachian Collection and with the Mt. Jefferson–New River State Park. The latter collection will be jointly held with the National Committee for the New River. Time will determine the value of the project.

REFERENCES

Albee, M. (1988) *South Fork New River Survey Study*. Draft report presented to the N.C. Department of Natural Resources and Community Development.

Daniel, T., and R. Boster. (1976) *Measuring Landscape Aesthetics: The Scenic Beauty Estimation Method*. USDA Forest Service Paper RM-167. Denver: Rock Mountain Experiment Station.

Goodman, W. (1968) *Principles and Practice of Urban Planning*. Washington, DC: International City Managers Association.

Schoenbaum, T. J. (1979) *The New River Controversy*. Winston-Salem, NC: J. F. Blair Publishing.

State of North Carolina. (1990) *An Assessment of the North Carolina Natural and Scenic Rivers System*. Raleigh, NC: Division of Parks and Recreation.

State of North Carolina. (1971) *North Carolina Natural and Scenic Rivers Act*. N.C. General Statute 113A Sects. 30-44.

Thompson, J. (1990) "New River Future Uncertain." *The Mountains Times*, 11(25):1, 14.

U.S. Congress. (1968) *National Wild and Scenic Rivers Act of 1968*. P. L. 90-542, as amended April 1977.

BIBLIOGRAPHY

Austin, S. (1987) *Land-Use Change Along the South Fork New River, North Carolina—1975-1987*. Unpublished thesis. Durham, NC: Duke University.

Smith, W. (1987) *The Problem of Regulating Development in the N.C. Mountains Along the New River*. Winston-Salem: N.C. Department of Natural Resources and Community Development, Division of Community Assistance.

State of North Carolina. (1977) *South Fork New River Study*. Raleigh, NC: N.C. Department of Natural Resources and Community Development.

USDI. (1976) *Final Environmental Impact Statement: Proposed South Fork New River National Wild and Scenic River, N.C.* Washington, DC: Bureau of Outdoor Recreation.

Venters, V. (1990) "Old River, New Trouble." *Wildlife in North Carolina, 54*(8): 8-15.

Roanoke River Corridor Study, Phases I and II

Helen Smythers

INTRODUCTION

Helen Smythers, Chief of Community Development for the Fifth Planning District Commission in Roanoke, Virginia: Recently, I served as the Project Manager for the Roanoke River Corridor Study. Three other PDCs also provided staff for this project West Piedmont, Central Virginia and New River Valley. The 7 participating localities were the Counties of Montgomery, Roanoke, Franklin, and Bedford, the Cities of Salem and Roanoke, and the Town of Vinton. The Smith Mountain Lake Policy Advisory Board also assisted. The smartest thing we did was to get the environmental and interest groups in on the study from the start. There were 22 of them and they gave me some great ideas, and they weren't afraid to get dirty and go out surveying the river with me.

AN INNOVATIVE COOPERATIVE STUDY

The Roanoke River Corridor Study is a multi-jurisdictional, multiregional cooperative study. The idea for the study originated in 1987, when the local planning commissions in the Roanoke Valley and the Fifth Planning District Commission began meeting together to discuss mutual needs. In 1988, the group recognized that the river could not be examined in a segmented fashion and that there would be numerous benefits in studying the river from its headwaters to Smith Mountain Lake. Therefore, the study area was expanded to include the other PDCs and counties.

The Virginia Environmental Endowment, Virginia Water Control Board, and participating PDCs funded the study and report preparation in 2 overlapping phases from December 1988 through September 1990. During this process, differing opinions were analyzed and compromises were sought. The result was the completion of a cooperative study representing the joint needs and recommendations of the river's diverse users. Since that time, the study has been under local government review. When each locality has taken action, the jurisdictions and PDCs will resume meeting to implement the recommendations.

STUDY AREA

The study area encompasses the Roanoke River (including North and South Forks) from its headwaters in Montgomery and Roanoke Counties through the Roanoke Valley to Hardy Ford Bridge at Smith Mountain Lake in Bedford and Franklin Counties. The length of the study area is approximately 80 miles and the width of the study corridor is generally 750 feet from the floodplain boundary on either side of the river. I imagine that many of you are familiar with the Chesapeake Bay Initiatives. Well, the Roanoke River Basin is not located in the Chesapeake Bay area; our study area is in southwest Virginia. Since we did not have the unifying influence of the Chesapeake Bay Act, our task was both more difficult and much easier. For example, localities looked more favorably on our ideas because they came from a grassroots effort and because the localities were involved every step of the way. I'll admit that adoption of the recommendations has taken up to a year in some jurisdictions, but overall, opposition has been slight.

A *Partnership for Beauty and Progress*   53

STUDY GOAL

The goal of the study was the documentation of existing conditions in the Roanoke River Corridor, with an emphasis on recommending ways in which identified problems, opportunities, and protection needs can be addressed. This was achieved through the cooperation of three committees—policy, technical, and citizen—as well as five open community workshops. The result is a comprehensive computerized river inventory and a set of short-term and long-term recommendations for public and private involvement.

SLIDES OF SURVEY FINDINGS

Numerous slides were taken while the planners surveyed the river corridor. (The following is the outline of captions for the slide show presented. Publishing limitations prohibits the inclusion of the slides here.)

1. ROANOKE RIVER CORRIDOR STUDY
2. The river as seen from a footbridge by Victory Stadium.
3. The North Fork as seen from Route 785 north of Luster's Gate.
4. LAND USE
5. An industry that is located in Roanoke County built up to the river's edge.
6. An industry in Salem that maintains an extensive vegetative buffer between the building and the river.
7. Outside storage in an older industrial area.
8. This is a newer industrial area (Blue Ridge Beverage) in Glenvar where more controls are in place.
9. Commercial use shown located on river's edge.
10. A commercial building in Roanoke City with a berm between the river and the building.
11. Residential use located along the river that shows erosion control of drainage.
12. Here's a single family home that maintains a buffer by the river.
13. A history of floods explains the need for this measuring sign under the bridge near Roanoke Memorial Hospital.
14. Recreational land is an excellent use of floodplain land. This is the River's Edge Sports Complex in Roanoke City.
15. This shot of a Dairy Farm on the North Fork shows the result of the lack of erosion controls.
16. Agriculture and grazing is located mostly on the North Fork of the river, but in Glenvar (Roanoke County) there are also a few farms.
17. Another agriculture use is the taking of water from the river to irrigate fields.
18. This shot shows how the bank is being undercut by the fluvial processes of the river.
19. This slide is near Blacksburg Country Club and shows an erosional control provided by the Rip Rap on the meander bend.
20. This is on the North Fork where cattle are allowed to graze along the bank.
21. Same practice but located on the South Fork.
22. This slide shows a natural state of the bank. Notice the fence along the bank to keep farm animals away from the river.
23. This slide shows the lack of erosion controls for the drainage exiting from this dairy farm. These soils are excessively eroded.
24. This farm maintains a thick buffer from the river.
25. Litter is a problem almost every where along the river. This litter is thrown from the roadside into river.

26. There is litter near the river here where route 636 crosses the South Fork.
27. Community cleanup activities help correct litter problems. This is a cleanup crew outside Tweeds on Clean Valley Day.
28. This is treated sewage entering the North Fork from Blacksburg Country Club.
29. This is the water intake for the City of Salem.
30. This is a shot of the train derailment of April 20, 1990, near Ironto.
31. This is a shot about 3 to 4 miles downstream from the derailment where farmers are trying to keep cattle from entering the river. A hay barrier is in the foreground to catch some of the oil spill.
32. This is a scenic picture down on the river below the river derailment.
33. ACCESS
34. This is in Roanoke City in Wasena Park. The sign tells of hazards in this part of the river.
35. Just a few hundred feet downstream, men are fishing for trout recently stocked in the river.
36. More recreation in Wasena Park.
37. This is a playground in Norwich.
38. Here is a picture on the North Fork that shows a fence blocking passage on the river.
39. Further downstream on the North Fork, in a very navigable part of the river, barbed wire is strung across the river to deter cattle.
40. ENVIRONMENT
41. A refrigerator is seen here near Shawsville Elementary School. A hazard no doubt.
42. A beautiful shot of the South Fork marred by debris dumped into the river from the roadside.
43. The debris in the previous slide is shown here in its proximity to the road.
44. Limiting access may help reduce illegal dumping.
45. As will public trash cans.
46. This slide shows erosion of the bank, possibly natural.
47. This extensive use of rip-rap and a pipe prevents further erosion to a previously damaged section of bank.
48. Drainage from a commercial and residential area, notice the erosion caused by the runoff.
49. Close-up shot of the drainage from previous slide.
50. This is a paved drainage way.
51. Runoff in the urban area.
52. Green Hill Park in Roanoke County uses grassed drainage ways to direct runoff.
53. Another shot of Green Hill Park.
54. This area near Lafayette is used as a pull off from the road to dump debris on the bank of the river.
55. This is a tributary behind the previous junk pile that is thoroughly littered.
56. In Salem, some popular river access points were blocked to vehicles in order to reduce littering from cars.
57. This is a large dump in Montgomery County near the Roanoke County line. Its length is about 70 yards long.
58. This picture shows that its height is about 15 to 2 feet. It is only 10 to 20 yards from the river.
59. Illegal dumping was less of a problem in areas where house-to-house collection is provided—these are Salem's trash containers.
60. CULTURAL RESOURCES
61. Here we have the rural setting that is characteristic of lands along the North Fork of the Roanoke River.
62. This is also on the North Fork in Ellett Valley.
63. North Fork again.

64. Even in the urban areas, quiet family homes by the river are a prized way of life.
65-69. I want to leave you with some images of the beauty of the river—both in the more isolated areas and in the urban areas.

RECOMMENDATIONS

Following completion of the river inventory, recommendations for future action were made. First, we ask that each locality formally adopt the Roanoke River Corridor Study as a part of its Comprehensive Plan, and appoint a planner to serve on a commission that will help implement the recommendations. That group, tentatively called the Roanoke River Conservation District Commission, should have its first meeting by late 1991. We anticipate that, among other things, a conservation overlay zone will result from this future planning work. This overlay would be presented to each locality for consideration and adoption. It might include such things as:

a. limitations on the development and use of lands lying within the corridor overlay zone
b. compliance with Best Management Practices for all uses and development undertaken in the zone
c. establishment and/or retention of minimum vegetative buffer areas along the riverbank
d. soil and erosion measures for all land disturbance activities in the zone
e. performance criteria for land development planned within the zone

SUMMARY

Compared to some of the presentations you will hear at this conference, we are closer to the beginning than we are to the end of a long, complex process. Our goal, protection of the Roanoke River Corridor, may take decades. However, I am dedicated to the goal and willing to put in the time needed. Wish us luck. And thank you for listening.

An Interactive Recreation Demand/Supply Model for Personal Computers

Herman F. Senter and James P. Jarvis

ABSTRACT

A revised model for estimating demand/supply relationships for outdoor recreation activities within a geographic region is discussed. Data requirements to operate the model and output reports of analyses are explained. Use of the menu-driven interactive model software (for IBM-compatible PC's) to perform various analyses is illustrated. Current applications of the model for needs analysis and planning in a statewide context are described.

INTRODUCTION

The recreation demand/supply model RDSM discussed below is the fourth generation of a model initially developed for the U.S. Army Corps of Engineers [1, 2]. The original model (Version 1.0) was subsequently modified for use by South Carolina's Department of Parks, Recreation, and Tourism (SCPRT) and the Georgia Department of Natural Resources (GDNR) [3]. The development of an interactive software code for IBM compatible personal Computers (Version 3.0) was reported in [6].

The current edition of the RDSM software, Version 4.0, was created to facilitate its application by GDNR. It is used by GDNR for inventory record keeping, needs analyses, exploratory research analyses, and report generation. The Version 4.0 software is menu-driven and self-instructing; thus, little or no training is required for routine analyses.

RDSM requires baseline data on recreation activities, population-based demand for those activities, and the available recreation supply within the study region. Demand is distributed on a site-by-site basis according to travel distance factors. Analyses are done activity-by-activity for the years specified. RDSM (remand projection methodology is based on projected population growth and expected trends in future participation. Estimates of demand and supply are expressed in units of activity occasions per prime season weekend day.

RDSM consists of three main modules: 1) a demand estimator; 2) a supply inventory; and 3) an allocation procedure. These are shown schematically in Figure 1 (see also [3]). Factors affecting demand, supply, and the allocation process are indicated in the figure. Basic information items needed to quantify these factors are listed in Table 1. These are discussed below.

BASELINE DATA REQUIREMENTS

Initially a *study region* (or *market area*) is determined; for example, a state. The region is partitioned into *demand centers* for which base year population estimates and growth projections are available. These centers might be counties within a state, or in a more detailed analysis, census districts. For each activity to be studied, per capita participation rates are required, together with information on willingness-to-travel for that activity.

The study region is also partitioned into *supply sites* which may be single facilities or aggregates of several facilities within a locality. Supply sites and demand centers need not be identical. The amount of supply for an activity at a site is based on the quantity of facilities at the site, their carving capacities and the activity turnover rates. This information constitutes a supply inventory for the study region.

Travel times, distances, or costs between each demand center supply site pair must be specified. They are used in conjunction with willingness-to-travel factors to allocate the demand to supply. For each activity, travel time zones and corresponding preferences must be estimated from survey data. Figure 2 (see also [3]) provides an illustration of four travel-time zones. The number and sizes of the zones, and the travel factors Pi and p;, depend on the particular activity. For example, most individuals are unwilling to travel far to play tennis (Ply small), while campers usually prefer to travel some minimum distance from home (pi' large).

Factors to account for differences in activity participation rates between urban and rural demand centers and to allow for out-of-region demand are optional. Likewise, supply site attractiveness ratings are optional.

For reporting purposes, analysts may wish to aggregate demand centers or supply sites, perhaps by geographic subregions such as planning districts within a state. Information about desired groupings must be provided.

As an example, GDNR uses RDSM for statewide demand/supply analysis. Demand centers are the 159 counties which are also the supply sites. Baseline data is maintained for 14 outdoor activities. U.S. Bureau of the Census county population figures are used together with Georgia's population projections and participation rates to estimate demand. Supply information is updated as changes in facilities occur to maintain an accurate inventory of supply for each activity and county. Analyses are reported by county, by planning district (five), and for the entire state.

OPTIONS AND OUTPUTS

To analyze a particular activity, the model user must select the activity and the year of the analysis. RDSM reports *total demand, met demand, unmet demand, used supply, residual supply* and *potential usage* by demand center, by supply site, by subregion, and for the entire study region. These measures are in units of activity occasions per prime season weekend day.

Alternatively, the user may elect to analyze all activities for a single demand center or supply site. Other options permit the user to change baseline data such as participation rates or supply inventory. An unspecified a blank" activity is provided to facilitate study of the effects of adding a new activity to the list of existing ones. Unless specifically designated, changes in baseline data are not permanent, existing only for a single session of model use.

Some principal features of RDSM are illustrated by the samples of screen output which follow.

Program execution is initiated by entering the command RDSM. A start up screen (Figure 3) is displayed while the software reads the required baseline data. When initialization is complete, the user may proceed to the **Main Menu** (Figure 4).

Items (1) - (4) of the Main Menu are used to revise baseline information. Data changes can be temporary, for simulation purposes, or permanent for inventory updating. Options (6) or (7) may be selected to specify the kind of activity analysis desired.

For illustration purposes, suppose the user chooses to analyze a specific activity. Entry of main menu option (7) brings up the **Activity Selection Menu** (Figure 5). All activities provided in the baseline data are listed as well as a *blank activity* which may be used to introduce a new activity, either temporarily or permanently. Figure 5 illustrates the procedure for analyzing an existing activity, Text Camping, for the year 1985. Effects of competition for facilities by out-of-state users are excluded, while site attractiveness effects on demand are considered.

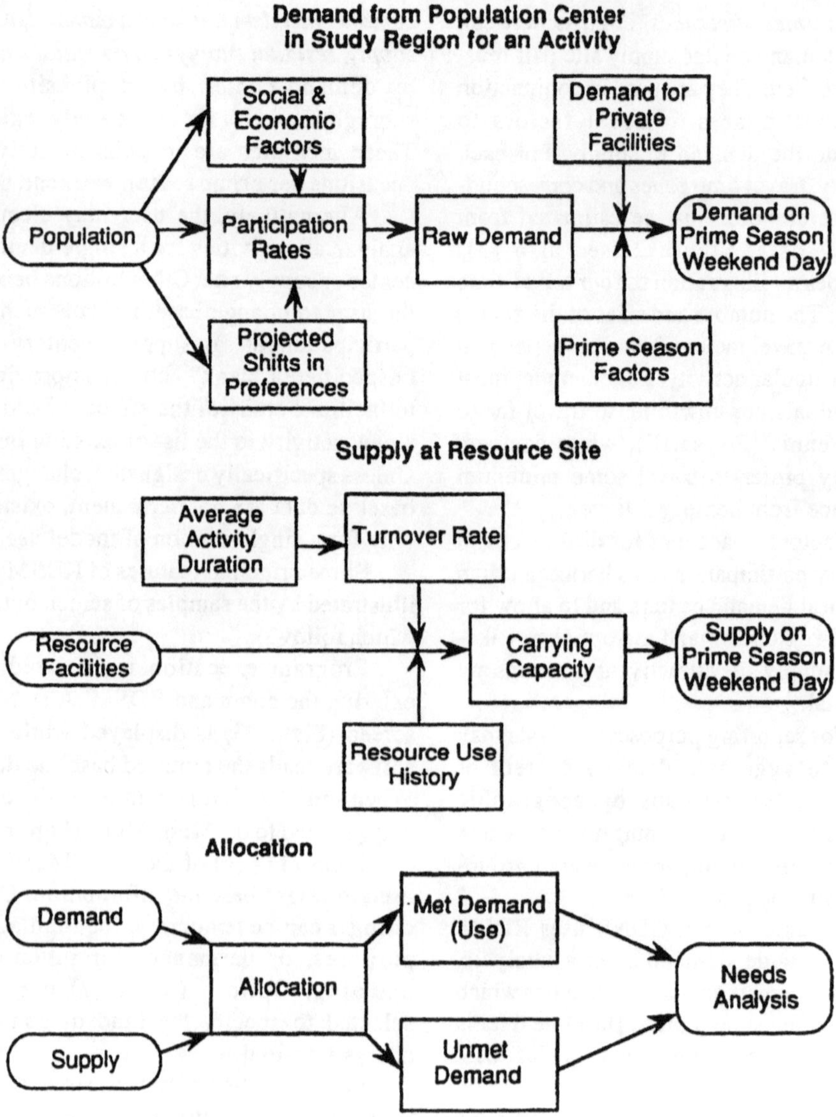

Demand from Population Center in Study Region for an Activity

[Diagram: Population → Social & Economic Factors, Participation Rates, Projected Shifts in Preferences → Raw Demand → (with Demand for Private Facilities and Prime Season Factors) → Demand on Prime Season Weekend Day]

Supply at Resource Site

[Diagram: Average Activity Duration → Turnover Rate; Resource Facilities, Turnover Rate, Resource Use History → Carrying Capacity → Supply on Prime Season Weekend Day]

Allocation

[Diagram: Demand and Supply → Allocation → Met Demand (Use) and Unmet Demand → Needs Analysis]

Figure 1. Three modules comprising RDSM

After pausing for activity analysis computations, RDSM returns to a modified main menu which included the additional item (8) shown in Figure 6. Entry of this report option brings up the **Report Menu** of Figure 7. (If output is directed to a printer or a file, a tenth option, "All of the above," appears.) Reports generated by selections of items (1) - (7) of the Report Menu are shown in Figures 8 - 15 respectively.

To illustrate the procedure for changing baseline data, suppose option (1) of the **Main Menu** (Figure 4), "1. Display or Change activity data" is selected. The user is prompted to choose an activity, after which the data for that activity is displayed (Figure 16).

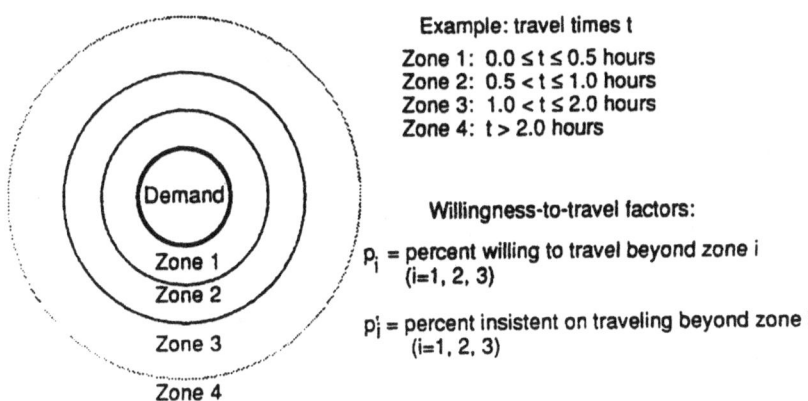

Figure 2. Example of travel time zones.

The preceding figures illustrate some analyses, procedures, and features of RDSM. The software is self-documented and assumes no prior instruction of the user. Experience has shown that novices can readily follow the menu instructions to produce the reports they desire. The software includes a variety of safeguards against entry of invalid data (such as a negative participation rate) or accidental erasure of baseline information. Further information about RDSM is provided in the *RDSM User's Guide* [5]. Details about the software and about data specifications are given in the *RDSM Technical Reference* [4].

CURRENT APPLICATIONS

Version 4.0 of RDSM is used by GDNR for analysis, planning, and report production. By updating changes in recreation facilities, a current site-by-site inventory of supply is maintained. The model enables

```
                Recreation Demand-Supply Model
                       Version 4.0 (1990)

                           prepared for
               Georgia Department of Natural Resources
                   Parks & Historic Sites Division

                               by
                      Upstate Resources, Inc.
                          P.O. Box 152
                        Six Mile, SC  29682

Reading data and initializing system.
One moment please...

Reading activity rate data
Reading population data
Reading travel time data
Reading supply inventory data
Reading out-of-state usage data
Reading site attractiveness data
Reading regional aggregation data
Initialization complete.

Press any key to continue...
```

Figure 3. Initialization Screen

```
              Recreation Demand/Supply Model v4.0   (URI-1990)

     Main Menu

 0) End this session

 1) Display or Change activity data
 2) Display or Change supply data
 3) Display or Change population data
 4) Display or Change groups for Demand Areas and Supply Sites

 5) Change report destination (Screen, Printer, File)
         (currently: Screen)

 6) Analyze all activities for a single demand area/supply site
 7) Analyze a specific activity

 Enter a number between     0 and     7 and press return:
```

Figure 4. Main Menu

```
              Recreation Demand/Supply Model v4.0   (URI-1990)

     Choose an activity.

 0) Return to main menu

 1) Tent Camping         2) Golf                 3) Tennis
 4) Trailer Camping      5) Lake Fishing         6) Motor Boating
 7) Pool Swimming        8) Basketball           9) Football
10) Baseball            11) Bicycling           12) Trailbike Riding
13) Day Hiking          14) Lake Swimming       15) Blank Activity

Enter a number between     0 and    15 and press return:1

Do you wish to include the effects of out of state usage (Y/N)?n
Do you wish to include the effects of site attractiveness (Y/N)?y

Enter the year for which the model is to be run (1985-1995).
Enter a number between  1985 and  1995 and press return:1985
```

Figure 5. Activity Selection Menu

```
            Recreation Demand/Supply Model v4.0   (URI-1990)

    Main Menu

0) End this session

1) Display or Change activity data
2) Display or Change supply data
3) Display or Change population data
4) Display or Change groups for Demand Areas and Supply Sites

5) Change report destination (Screen, Printer, File)
        (currently: Screen)

6) Analyze all activities for a single demand area/supply site
7) Analyze a specific activity
8) Produce reports for activity: Tent Camping

Enter a number between      0 and      8 and press return:
```

Figure 6. Main Menu with Report Option

```
            Recreation Demand/Supply Model v4.0   (URI-1990)

    Choose the report to be generated for activity: Tent Camping

0) Return to main menu

1) Statewide summary
2) Regional demand summary
3) Regional supply summary
4) Planning district demand summary
5) Planning district supply summary
6) Demand area summary
7) Supply site summary
8) Usage for each demand area-supply site pair
9) Potential usage for each demand area-supply site pair

Enter a number between      0 and      9 and press return:
```

Figure 7. Report Menu

```
          Recreation Demand/Supply Model v4.0    (URI-1990)

Statewide Summary of Demand and Supply for 1985
     Activity:    Tent Camping
     Supply units: Sites
Includes effects of site attractiveness

(Values given in supply units per prime season weekend day)

Total demand                                    5367.
Demand for public, designated facilities        3489.
Demand for other facilities                     1878.
Total supply inventory                          3057.

Met demand                                      1790.
Unmet demand                                    1699.
Residual supply                                 1267.

Press: E to Exit...
```

Figure 8. Statewide Demand and Supply Report

```
          Recreation Demand/Supply Model v4.0    (URI-1990)

  Demand summary for Geographical Region
  Year: 1985      Activity: Tent Camping    Supply units: Sites
  Includes effects of site attractiveness
  (Values in supply units per prime season weekend day)
```

Demand Area	Total Demand	Met Demand	Unmet Demand
Totals	3489.	1790.	1699.
Mountains	486.	304.	182.
Metro	1172.	405.	767.
Central	868.	493.	375.
Southwest	401.	235.	166.
Southeast	338.	214.	124.
Coastal	223.	138.	85.

```
  Press: E to Exit...
```

Figure 9. Geographic Region Demand Report

```
            Recreation Demand/Supply Model v4.0   (URI-1990)

   Supply summary for Geographical Region
   Year: 1985      Activity: Tent Camping      Supply units: Sites
   Includes effects of site attractiveness
   (Values in supply units per prime season weekend day)

Supply                        Total      Used      Residual    Potential
Area                          Supply     Supply    Supply      Usage
-----------------------------------------------------------------------
Totals                        3057.      1790.     1267.

Mountains                      810.       507.      303.       1527.
Metro                          173.       173.        0.        909.
Central                        849.       520.      329.       1455.
Southwest                      230.       211.       19.        434.
Southeast                      718.       298.      420.        530.
Coastal                        277.        80.      197.        284.

   Press: E to Exit...
```

Figure 10. Geographic Region Supply Report

```
            Recreation Demand/Supply Model v4.0   (URI-1990)

   Demand summary for Planning Area
   Year: 1985      Activity: Tent Camping      Supply units: Sites
   Includes effects of site attractiveness
   (Values in supply units per prime season weekend day)

Demand                        Total           Met           Unmet
Area                          Demand          Demand        Demand
-----------------------------------------------------------------------
Totals                        3489.           1790.         1699.

Coosa Valley                   219.             72.          147.
North Georgia                  114.            107.            7.
Georgia Mountains              153.            125.           28.
Atlanta Regional              1172.            405.          767.
Northeast Georgia              147.             97.           50.
Chattahoochee-Flint            108.             44.           64.
McIntosh Trail                 143.             73.           70.
Oconee                          62.             46.           17.
Cent. Savannah River           223.             90.          133.

   Press: L for Last, N for Next, E to Exit...
```

Figure 11. Planning Area Demand Report

```
         Recreation Demand/Supply Model  v4.0   (URI-1990)

   Supply summary for Planning Area
   Year: 1985       Activity: Tent Camping     Supply units: Sites
   Includes effects of site attractiveness
   (Values in supply units per prime season weekend day)

 Supply                        Total        Used      Residual    Potential
 Area                          Supply       Supply    Supply      Usage
 ----------------------------------------------------------------------------
 Totals                        3057.        1790.     1267.

 Coosa Valley                   114.          98.       16.         674.
 North Georgia                   84.          84.        0.         176.
 Georgia Mountains              612.         325.      287.         677.
 Atlanta Regional               173.         173.        0.         909.
 Northeast Georgia               30.          30.        0.         230.
 Chattahoochee-Flint             56.          56.        0.         149.
 McIntosh Trail                  67.          67.        0.         483.
 Oconee                         178.         125.       53.         247.
 Cent. Savannah River            74.          64.       10.         166.

   Press: L for Last, N for Next, E to Exit...
```

Figure 12. Planning Area Supply Report

```
         Recreation Demand/Supply Model  v4.0   (URI-1990)

   Demand summary for Demand Areas
   Year: 1985       Activity: Tent Camping     Supply units: Sites
   Includes effects of site attractiveness
   (Values in supply units per prime season weekend day)

 Demand                        Total         Met              Unmet
 Area                          Demand        Demand           Demand
 ----------------------------------------------------------------------------
 Totals                        3489.         1790.            1699.

 Appling                         10.            7.               2.
 Atkinson                         4.            4.               0.
 Bacon                            6.            4.               2.
 Baker                            2.            2.               0.
 Baldwin                         22.           22.               0.
 Banks                            5.            4.               1.
 Barrow                          14.            8.               6.
 Bartow                          26.            7.              19.
 Ben Hill                        10.           10.               0.

   Press: L for Last, N for Next, E to Exit...
```

Figure 13. Demand Area Report

```
          Recreation Demand/Supply Model v4.0   (URI-1990)

   Supply summary for Supply Sites
   Year: 1985      Activity: Tent Camping      Supply units: Sites
   Includes effects of site attractiveness
   (Values in supply units per prime season weekend day)

Supply                             Total      Used      Residual   Potential
Area                              Supply     Supply      Supply      Usage
---------------------------------------------------------------------------
Totals                            3057.      1790.       1267.

Appling                             20.        20.          0.         35.
Atkinson                             0.         0.          0.          0.
Bacon                               35.        35.          0.         38.
Baker                                0.         0.          0.          0.
Baldwin                             47.        47.          0.        125.
Banks                                0.         0.          0.          0.
Barrow                               0.         0.          0.          0.
Bartow                              33.        33.          0.        215.
Ben Hill                             0.         0.          0.          0.

   Press: L for Last, N for Next, E to Exit...
```

Figure 14. Supply Site Report

```
          Recreation Demand/Supply Model v4.0   (URI-1990)

Actual Usage    for a demand area-supply site pair
Year: 1985      Activity: Tent Camping      Supply units: Sites
Includes effects of site attractiveness
(Values in supply units per prime season weekend day)

Demand Area    :    Appling
Supply Site    :    Atkinson
Actual Usage   :        0.

Press: E to Exit...
```

Figure 15. Usage between a Particular Demand Area–Supply Site Pair

```
                Recreation Demand/Supply Model v4.0   (URI-1990)

        Activity Participation Rate Data
        Choose an item to change

     0) Return to main menu

     1) Activity name: Tent Camping
     2) Supply unit name: Sites
     3) Fraction of population participating                       0.1210
     4) Number of activity occasions per participant per year      1.8000
        Overall participation rate (activity occasions per year)   0.2178
     5) Fraction of activity on a prime season weekend day         0.0145
     6) Fraction of activity at public, designated facilities      0.6500
     7) Urban-rural ratio                                          1.0300
     8) Average carrying capacity of a supply unit                 3.5000
     9) Average daily turnover rate                                1.0000
        Capacity standard (activity occasions per unit per day)    3.5000
    10) Copy willingness-to-travel factors from another activity

     Enter a number between     0 and    10 and press return:
```

Figure 16. Activity Participation Rate Report

the recreation planner to simulate the relative effects of various changes in the recreation system, such as shifts in supply, demand, participation rates, site attractiveness, etc. For example, the impact on met demand resulting from closing of facilities at specified supply cites due to operating budget cuts can be studied. Population projections provide a means for anticipating future demand and corresponding supply location needs. The model produces relative measures of demand and use on a county-by-county basis which serve as a guide to allocation of state recreation funds among the countries.

Demand and supply figures computed by the model may not coincide with actual use on prime season weekend days and must be interpreted by the analyst on the basis of experience and by comparison of relative effects. Attempts to validate model outputs, or to scale activity estimates to correspond with observed use, have been hindered by the absence of actual use data.

CONCLUSION

The discussion of RDSM in this report illustrates some principal features of the model software and describes its use as a tool for statewide outdoor recreation planning and analysis. Application need not be limited to that setting. The general structure of the model invites its adaptation to analogous situations where demand and supply can be measured and a "cost" or penalty (reward) function for assigning demand to supply can be defined. One purpose of this paper is to describe Version 4.0 of RDSM in the context of its current use. A second purpose is to invite consideration of other applications of this model for recreation planning and analysis. Suggestions for changes or improvements in the modeling concepts are sought. Comments or discussion regarding the software are welcome.

Table 1.
Information factors required for each module of RDSM

I. *Factors Related to Demand Estimation*
 1. study region: geographic region and its subdivisions
 2. population estimates and projections
 3. activities
 4. units of measurement: activity occasions, visitor hours, etc.
 5. time of measurement (e.g., prime season weekend day)
 6. standards
   a. participation rate (% participating and frequency)
   b. trends in participation
   c. fraction of participation during prime season
   d. fraction of participation on weekend days
   e. urban-rural participation rate factor
 7. demand served by "undesignated" facilities
 8. demand served by non-public facilities
 9. demand arising outside the geographic region

II. *Factors Related to Supply Inventory*
 1. designation of supply region
 2. location of each enterprise site
 3. activities per enterprise
 4. carrying capacity
 5. attractiveness

III. *Factors Related to Allocation Decisions*
 1. travel zones
 2. willingness-to-travel
 3. attractiveness weights

REFERENCES

1. J. P. Jarvis, P. R. Saunders, and H. F. Senter. "Forecasting Recreation Demand in the Upper Savannah River Basin," *Annals of Tourism Research 8*, 236^256 (1981).

2. J. P. Jarvis and H. F. Senter. "A Model for Outdoor Recreation Planning," *The Clemson University Review of Industrial Management and Textile Science* 18:2, 71-76 (1979).

3. J. P. Jarvis and H. F. Senter. "Evaluating Outdoor Recreation Alternatives," National Outdoor Recreation Trends Symposium, Asheville, NC, 89-97 (1980).

4. J. P. Jarvis and H. F. Senter. *Recreation Demand/Supply Model (version 4.0): Technical Reference.* Upstate Resources, Inc., Six Mile, SC, 1990.

5. J. P. Jarvis and H. F. Senter. *Recreation Demand/Supply Model (version 4.0): User's Guide.* Upstate Resources, Inc., Six Mile, SC, 1990.

6. J. P. Jarvis, H. F. Senter, and T. Yearwood. "Applications of an Interactive Supply-Demand Model," Southeastern Recreation Research Conference, Asheville, NC, 7-18 (1987).

The Use of Computer Animation in Developing Interpretive Facilities Along the San Juan Skyway

James L. Sipes and Richard F. Ostergaard

The San Juan Skyway, located in southwest Colorado, traverses some of the most spectacular, rugged, and primitive country in all America. The Skyway is a 232 mile loop that connects the historic mountain towns of Durango, Silverton, Ouray, Telluride, and Cortez. The route has been described as an outstanding showcase of some of the most dynamic and spectacular rugged scenery in the nation and is often referred to as "The Most Scenic Drive in America." It was designated by the State of Colorado Scenic Byway Commission as the state's first State Scenic and Historic Byway. The Skyway is also one of three United States Forest Service Scenic Byways selected for the Department of Transportation's use of grant money made available by the 1989 Scenic Byways Study Act. A scenic byway is a travel route which traverses a scenic corridor of outstanding aesthetic, cultural, historic, or interpretive forest values. Also, within the Forest Service system, the forests charged with the development of the byway were designated as "Centers of Design Excellence" with the purpose of demonstrating "how to do it" for others developing scenic byways programs. One "how to" project involves the use of computer animation to develop interpretive facilities along the San Juan Skyway.

Forty-nine sites along the San Juan Skyway have been identified as locations for proposed interpretive facilities. The dominant interpretive themes are spectacular scenery, forest management activities, historic mining districts, geological formations, fall colors, ancient cultural ruins, weather dynamics, and the early railroads. Interpretation will take the form of signs at designed pullouts or along the highway, naming certain features or mountain peaks, or telling the story of a point of interest.

A series of three basic modules were developed for the proposed interpretive facilities. The first module is a "camera point" that consist of a small viewing deck and parking for two or three cars. The other two modules are much larger and more complex. A "standard" module consists of a viewing deck intended for 15 to 25 people and provides parking for five cars and two RVs. An "expanded" module (Figure 1) has essentially the same layout, but the viewing deck will hold 30 to 40 people and parking space is available for eight cars and three RVs.

Common to the "standard" and "expanded" modules is a staging area on the walkway between the parking areas. Within the staging area, the design provides for a large landscape rock sunk partially into the concrete. A plaque attached to the rock gives credit to the partnership responsible for the facility construction. Each module was designed to be relatively maintenance free, to provide the stated interpretive opportunities and to aesthetically fit the landscape. The modules will be adapted from one site to another, as necessary to fit site conditions.

The public has high expectations regarding the planning and development for interpretive facilities along the San Juan Skyway. Interpretive opportunities can greatly aid in the enjoyment and experience of the visitor, but only if the proposed interpretive facilities enhance, rather than detract from the surrounding landscapes. To adequately determine the impact of

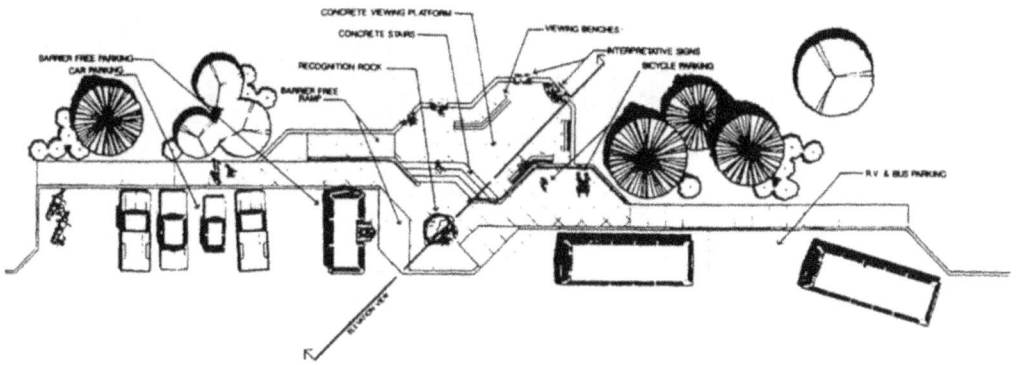

Figure 1. Expanded Plan

these proposed interpretive facilities on these surrounding landscapes, 3-D computer-generated models of the basic interpretive modules were constructed (Figure 2). These computer-generated models and animation sequences will greatly aid in future efforts to develop possible partnerships with service organizations and interest groups along the route.

3-DIMENSIONAL MODELING

To create 3-D computer models of the interpretive facilities, traditional hand-drawn maps were digitized using AutoCAD release 11. The digitized lines and arcs were combined to create polylines and exported as a DXF file into 3D Studio (Autodesk Inc.), a three-dimensional modeling tool that provides sophisticated animation as well. 3D Studio is composed of six modules that provide the capability for modeling, rendering, and scene-description: 2D Shaper, 3D Lofter, 3D Editor, Materials Editor, Renderer and Keyframer.

The DXF files were imported into the 2D Shaper module and converted the polylines into two-dimensional "shapes" which were lofted in the 3D Lofter module to create three-dimensional objects. In this manner, simple rectangles were projected up to create the retaining walls that defined the edges of the viewing decks for the interpretive facilities. The same method was used to create the benches, steps, curbs, sidewalks, and signage.

The most time-consuming task in 3-D animation is building the 3-D models which form the foundation of the sequences. A mathematical model of a building, a site, a retaining wall, or an interpretive facility can often be built or modified in far less time and at less cost than it takes to build a physical model with comparable accuracy. However, it should not be overlooked that 3-D modeling can be a laborious, repetitive task and intricate 3-D shapes can create special problems for the modeler. Traditional modeling methods can be used, but are time consuming and do not adapt well to objects with complicated shapes - such as trees and topography - that were a necessity to create the surrounding landscapes for the interpretive facilities. (Hoffman and Teeple, 1990)

Other software packages provide alternative ways to create 3-D objects. One method is to create simple geometric shapes such as cubes, cylinders, spheres, cones, and rectangles and combine them to create more complex objects. To create the trees surrounding the viewing decks, a black cone was constructed and turned upside-down. Numerous rectilinear plates were constructed and placed over the cone

Figure 2.

to created the layered appearance of evergreen trees. The surrounding landform consists of thousands of thin rectangles rotated in space and joined at the edges (Figure 3).

ADDING A TOUCH OF REALISM

The ability to create 3-D computer models is important, but it is the ability to make them look realistic that is so beneficial. A major difficulty with 3-D models is a lack of detail and the "cartoonish" appearance of the final images. Without taking a lot of time to add details, the computer-based models would be limited to use as study models. To add an acceptable level of detail and realism, 3D Studio texture mapping provides the Renderer module and the Materials Editor.

3D Studio's Materials Editor applies surface and light-reflective characteristics to an object and adds a touch of realism. Bump mapping, surface properties, and texture mapping all affect an object's appearance. Bump-mapping creates the appearance of roughness on a surface. Surface properties refer to the degree of transparency of and object and the way its surface reflects light and objects around it. In texture mapping an image of a texture, material, or object is overlaid on a 3-D computer model of an object. This image can be drawn by the designer with a paint system, but it is typically scanned from a photograph or a slide via an optical scanner. For example, a wood grain was captured and wrapped around a series of rectangles to help illustrate the benches in the viewing deck. The same technique was used to scan images of a specific site to create the background scenes.

The Renderer module allows the selection of settings for rendering and shading. After 3-D computer models of the interpretive facilities were constructed and materials defined, photorealistic color-shaded renderings of the models were produced under varied light conditions. The final renderings of the 3-D models were combined to create the illusion of animation. The final animation sequences simulate a series of visual experiences, such as those seen from a moving automobile (Figure 4).

ANIMATION

True animation requires that smooth, realistic movements be captured by the computer display. In traditional animation, 24 frames are typically displayed for every second of animation. Computer animation uses a slightly different standard of 30 frames per second. As a result, approximately 900 images are required to create a 30-second animation sequence showing a car driving past the interpretive facilities along the San Juan Skyway.

Computer animation has evolved because much of the repetitive work associated with traditional cell animation can now be accomplished quicker and easier using computer techniques. Traditional animation studios from the past, including Walt Disney, were often described as "sweat shops" where talented artists were subject to long hours of repetitive, monotonous tasks. Even the classic cartoons from the past were tedious for the animators who labored to create them. A 15-minute cartoon featuring Mickey Mouse, Donald Duck, Goofy, and the gang would contain approximately 30,000 drawings and might take a team of 20 skilled animators, artists, editors and checkers a month or more to produce. (Computer Images, 1986) Computers can simplify the animation process and speed it up dramatically.

Computer animation systems can be divided into three major categories: (1) electronic slide show, (2) 2D animation, and (3) 3D animation. (Anderson, 1989) Unlike true animation, an electronic slide show does not create the illusion of animation by rapidly displaying a series of images. Rather it creates the illusion of animation by providing smooth transitions from one image to the next. Two-dimensional programs simulates traditional frame-by-frame animation by combining sequences of images created with "paint" software. (Cudlitz, 1989)

3-D animation consists of creating simple geometric primitives such as rectangles, cylinders, and cones, combining these shapes to create more complex objects, and then moving around these objects. Three-dimensional (3-D) software

Figure 3.

Figure 4.

provides you with a wide range of choices for designing realistic models and creating simulations with real-world properties. 3-D animation has proved to be suitable for use by architects, but has not been utilized to the same degree by landscape architects. (Kinnucan, 1989)

LIMITATIONS

There are a number of reasons why the United States Forest Service and other organizations do not use computer animation. The primary reason is lack of knowledge by the users. Most designers have not been exposed to this technology, and acquiring this knowledge is difficult. In both the classroom and the office, learning to use computer animation software takes time away from an already busy agenda. As a result, most firms or organizations do not have anyone with the necessary skills or training to be proficient at creating three-dimensional computer animation sequences.

There are also a number of technical limitations. In terms of memory and processing power, animation is the most demanding computer graphics application. The amount of storage and processing power needed to create these types of sequences results in an expensive computer that falls outside the budget of most organizations or design firms. A typical PC-based animation system might include the animation software, a microcomputer with an 80386 or 80486 processor, a math coprocessor, 4 MB of RAM, a Targa video graphics board, an analog or composite monitor, a mouse or digitizer, an animation controller, and a good 3/4-inch tape deck. This system can be expected to cost approximately $25,000-$30,000. (Jadrnicek, 1988, pp. 70)

Another potential limitation is the final appearance of an animation sequence. The style and look of computer animation is noticeably different from that of traditional cel animation. (Vasilopoulos, 1990) If the final animation sequence is created by hand, we expect the quality to match that of the sequences created by Disney studios. If the final sequence is created via computer graphics, we compare these images to those we see on television. At the professional level of production, a 30-second commercial might take months to produce and typically has a budget of maybe $100,000 to $200,000. (Anderson, 1990, pp. 229) This is well beyond the resources of most organizations.

Only in the past few years have microcomputer animations been considered a feasible alternative to mainframe animations. In the area of quality, microcomputer animation has finally caught up to mainframe animations. (MacNicol, 1989) With the price of 3D hardware dropping and with PC systems beginning to add these types of 3D capabilities, landscape architects might find 3D computer modeling more appealing in the future. The ability to add motion via computer animation presents some interesting opportunities for conveying design alternatives such as the proposed interpretive facilities along the San Juan Skyway.

SOURCES

Computer Images. Time-Life Books Inc., Richmond, VA, 1986.

Cudlitz, Stuart. "Move It." *Macworld*, June 1989, pp. 108+.

Gantz, John. "The Changing Animation." *Computer Graphics World*, July 1988, Vol. 11, No. 7, pp. 25-28.

Harbison, Don. "Landscape Architects Tap CAD & GIS." *Computer Graphics World*, Vol. 11, No. 12, December, 1988, pp. 32-38.

Hoffman, E., Kenneth Hoffman, and Jon Teeple. *Computer Graphics Applications: An Introduction to Desktop Publishing & Design Presentation Graphics*, Wadsworth Publishing Company, Belmont, California: 1990, pp. 227-229.

Jadrnicek, Rik. "Architectural Animation." *Computer Graphics World*, April 1988, Vol. 11, No. 4, pp. 70-74.

Jadrnicek, Rik. "Bring a Project to Life with Animation." *CADENCE*, June 1990, Aerial Communications, Inc., pp. 71-73.

Kinnucan, Paul. "3-D Modeling Systems." *Computer Graphics Review*, Vol. 4, No. 9, September 1989, pp. 16-27.

MacNicol, Gregory. "A PC-Based Animation Primer." *Computer Graphics World*, November 1986, Vol. 9, No. 11, pp. 34-41.

MacNicol, Gregory. "PC Animation Gains Steam." *Computer Graphics World*, July 1988, Vol. 11, No. 7, pp. 50-55.

Robertson, Barbara. *Animation Goes to Work. Computer Graphics World*, July 1988, Vol. 11, No. 7, pp. 38-48.

Robertson, Barbara. "The Art of Improvisation." *Computer Graphics World*, December 1988, pp. 42-48.

Vasilopoulos, Audrey. "Cartoon Animation." *Computer Graphics World*, Vol. 13, No. 1, January 1990, pp. 77-80.

Metro Green: A Greenway Proposal for Kansas City

Stephanie A. Rolley

> ... to undertake important work in a halfhearted manner is the poorest economy, ... it is far better to plan comprehensively and broadly and proceed with actual construction leisurely, than to attempt economy in the original plans. Report of the Board of Park and Boulevard Commissioners Kansas City, Missouri 1893

One hundred years after the 1893 plan for Kansas City's parks and boulevards, tulle spirit of that plan has been resurrected. Approximately 230 miles of potential green way have been identified, mapped, and presented as an organizing framework for the increasingly dispersed metropolitan area. Rediscovering and building upon George Kessler's legacy, the plan offers a vision for Kansas City in the next century. This proposal, known as Metro Green, began early in 1990 as a community service project conducted by landscape architecture professionals and students. As the project grows, it promises to bring individuals and organizations across the city together in a variety of partnerships to implement the plan. The intent of his paper is to describe the historical context of Metro Green, to document work done to date and partnerships formed, and to discuss the future of the proposal.

HISTORICAL CONTEXT

In 1893, George Kessler, a landscape architect, and August Meyer, a civic leader, made a bold proposal for Kansas City's future. The result was a network of boulevards and parkways that structured the city's growth for almost 50 years. The system initially connected a number of small frontier settlements. Expansion of the system through the early 1900s provided a catalyst for the city's growth. The boulevards followed natural features rather than the existing street grid, creating graceful sweeping roadways that attracted residential development and preserved the natural environment. Kessler's plan serves as a model for planning which connects the natural and built environments. He recognized the benefits, both financial and aesthetic, of designing a city to enhance the natural environment.

The impact of the 1893 plan on Kansas City's form is undeniable. Kansas City was a vehicular oriented city long before the nationwide sub urbanization of America after World War II. Boulevards carried people, first by carriage and later by automobile, out into surrounding farmland and encouraged development of small suburban communities. The intent was to build a city low in density. As a result, downtown is primarily a symbolic center for business. Today, the majority of the city's business is conducted in suburban business centers and office parks. It was Kessler's plan which initially drew the city's growth away from the river and downtown, and, in doing so, established the suburban quality of the metropolitan area. During the past two decades Kansas City grew at unprecedented rates. The metropolitan area now encompasses eight counties, five of which are almost entirely urbanized. That five county area encompasses over 66 communities in two states. Home to 1.5 million people, Kansas City today is much more than the dusty frontier community for which Kessler planned. The political struggles he faced are multiplied many times over as jurisdictions overlap and conflict. The character of the land has changed as well. At the turn of the century, Kansas City was situated on land characterized by rolling hills and wooded slopes.

Today, the city stretches from the steep bluffs at the confluence of the Kansas and Missouri Rivers to the flat farmland of rural Kansas and Missouri. The beauty of the land within Kansas City's expanded limits is often subtle and less easily preserved than the area Kessler shaped.

THE PROCESS

Metro Green was developed as a gift to the host city of the Annual Meeting of the American Society of Landscape Architects (ASLA), Kansas City. Each year the local ASLA chapter in the city hosting the convention conducts a Community Assistance Team project. The program's intent is to provide visibility for the profession through community service. Past projects include a boulevard redevelopment plan in Baltimore, Maryland, a master plan for the Presidio in San Francisco, California, and a gateway design for Orlando, Florida. The scope, duration and final product of a CAT project is left to the local chapter, but all present solutions to a significant local community design problem. The 1991 Community Assistance Team was comprised of landscape architecture professionals in both the public and private sectors and students and faculty from Kansas State University. The team received special assistance from Philip Lewis, Jr., Director of the Environmental Awareness Center at the University of Wisconsin.

With the 1893 plan as inspiration, discussions about a potential ASLA Community Assistance Team (CAT) project began in April 1990. Members of the local ASLA chapter identified a short list of objectives:

- Identify areas where potential linkages and connections could be made between the park systems of different political jurisdictions.
- Develop a set of planning/design

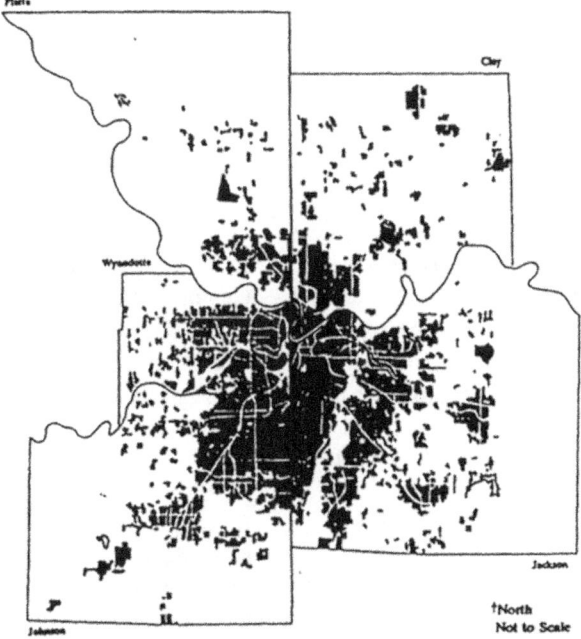

Source: 1989 Landis Aerial Photography

Figure 1. Urban Boundaries of the Kansas City Metropolitan Area

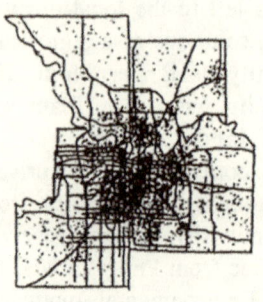 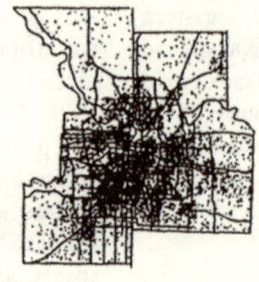 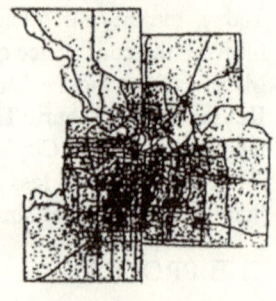

1970 KANSAS CITY METRO AREA POPULATION 1990 KANSAS CITY METRO AREA POPULATION 2010 KANSAS CITY METRO AREA PROJECTED POPULATION

Source: Mid-America Regional Council

Figure 2. Population Distribution in the Kansas City Metropolitan Area

guidelines for these areas of potential linkage and for other areas not included within existing park plans.
- Create a planning forum that would eventually be institutionalized and would foster the exchange of ideas and opinions among the region's park planners.

With these objectives as a general guide, a studio of Kansas State University landscape architecture students set out to explore Kansas City. While area and issue specific studies have been completed on a regular basis, there has not been a comprehensive study of Kansas City's physical characteristics in the past twenty years. The studio organized an unprecedented inventory of the five county metropolitan area to identify the urban boundaries, transportation patterns, significant landmarks and land use patterns, parks and designated open space, and slopes, woodlands, and stream corridors.

Urban Areas

Developed and undeveloped areas were mapped to determine the outer boundaries of urban Kansas City. The intent was to gain an understanding of Kansas City's actual boundaries. Rapid suburban growth during the 1980s outstripped most long range plans for communities on the city's fringe. The pattern that emerged is one of concentrated urbanization at the confluence of the rivers surrounded by fragmented development of former farmland. Figure 1 illustrates the impact of the natural environment on development. Northern and eastern metropolitan Kansas City, an area characterized by steep bluffs and dense vegetation, is divided by belts of open land. In contrast, the flat rural character of the southwestern area of the city facilitated development, resulting in an almost solid mass of urban form unbroken by open space. Figure 2 illustrates the rapid growth of suburban Kansas City during the past 20 years and projecting ahead 20 years. As projected, the continued expansion of Kansas City to the southwest could occur without relief imposed by the natural environment.

Transportation Patterns

In Kessler's plan, boulevards and parkways provided connections between small communities. A strong visual image of Kansas City, for visitors and residents alike, is often one of curving boulevards, wide medians and stately homes. In reality, that image is created by a very small part of Kansas City and the historic network forms a very small part of the city's transportation system. As engineers assumed responsibility for roadway design, boulevards and parkways became names of streets rather than roadway types. The 1893 report called for a network of roadways which would check the tendency to spread out. Today we have a network which facilitates our tendency to sprawl. The following figure illustrates the location of Kessler's 1893 network within contemporary transportation systems.

Landmarks and Land Use

Significant historic, cultural, entertainment and commercial landmarks were identified and mapped. Selected sites include regional attractions such as the Nelson Atkins Museum of Art, the Truman Sports Complex, and Worlds of Fun, as well as small, but significant, historic site and neighborhood shopping districts. In addition, general land use was mapped in the categories of commercial district, industrial areas, and residential districts. The intent was to gain an understanding of Kansas City's built form The map revealed a city of distinct communities. Although Kessler's historic network of roadways was not extended beyond the limits of Kansas City, Missouri, the city continued to grow as a series of small suburban communities in the pattern he established.

Parks and Designated Open Space

Cataloging all parks and designated open space in the five county area was a substantial part of the inventory. Recognizing that existing parks would probably provide the foundation for the yet to be selected Community Assistance Team project, this task was completed in a much more thorough and comprehensive way

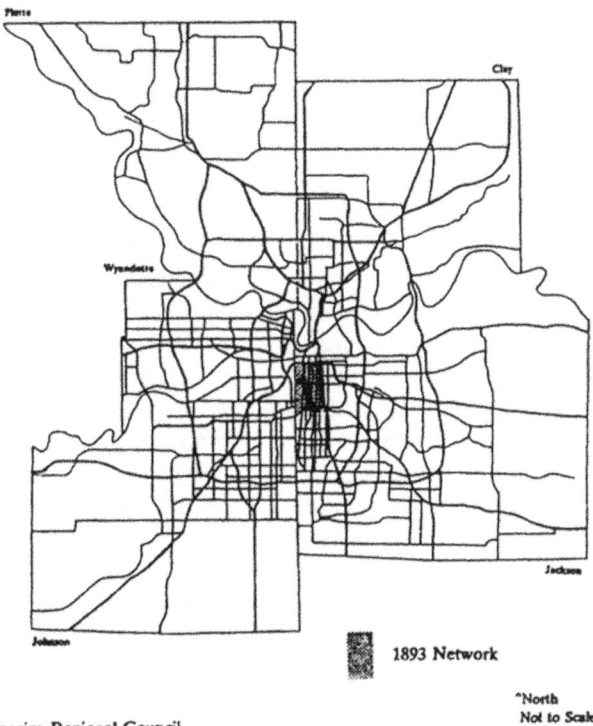

Source: Mid-America Regional Council

Figure 3. Transportation Systems in the Kansas City Metropolitan Area

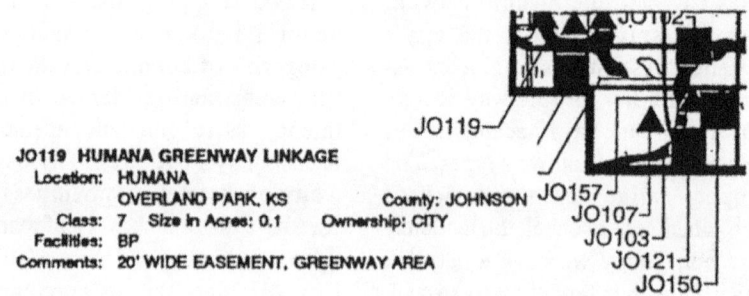

JO119 HUMANA GREENWAY LINKAGE
Location: HUMANA
OVERLAND PARK, KS   County: JOHNSON
Class: 7   Size in Acres: 0.1   Ownership: CITY
Facilities: BP
Comments: 20' WIDE EASEMENT, GREENWAY AREA

Source: Kansas State University, Department of Landscape Architecture

Figure 4. Park Inventory of the Kansas City Metropolitan Area

than the other inventory factors. The inventory of over 600 parks is contained in a freestanding document providing a summary of each park's location, size, classification, and facilities. (See Figure 4) Analysis of the inventory revealed a number of existing connections between individual parks. Linear parks of one mile to over fifteen miles in length are part of several municipal and county park systems.

Slopes, Woodlands and Stream Corridors

It was the Kansas and Missouri Rivers which attracted the Kansa and Osage Indians and, later, trappers and settlers to the area. In the early 1900s, as development followed the boulevard system, Kansas City turned its back on the rivers. Today, the shorelines are lined by industrial uses, often making the rivers inaccessible and unattractive. The two rivers are fed by dozens of tributary rivers, creeks and streams contained within five major watersheds. The majority of tree masses are found near streams or concentrations of water. Similarly, slopes over 12.5 percent are usually found adjacent to waterways. In the north and east, wooded bluffs wind along the streamways. In southwest and west Kansas City, the mixture of agriculture land and grassland bordered by wooded creeks creates a much different environment.

ANALYSIS

With a comprehensive inventory in place, the studio set about locating a specific linear park project for the ASLA local chapter to adopt as the 1991 CAT project. Synthesis of the inventory revealed a series of potential connections far greater in scale than originally anticipated. Instead of one linkage or one connection between a Kessler boulevard and a modern boulevard, the group discovered a concentric pattern of open land composed of an inner loop of approximately 90 miles and an outer loop of approximately 140 miles. The team had hoped to find potential connections between existing parks. Instead, the possibility of a system that could link much more than single parks was revealed. A proposal for a comprehensive green way system, Metro Green, was selected as the 1991 CAT project.

Examination of the inner loop reveals the rich topography and vegetation of the heart of Kansas City. Although suburban growth pushed beyond the inner green belt, it has remained relatively unthreatened. The land simply did not allow development. As a result, much of the southern portion of the inner loop is already a part of municipal and county park systems. In Jackson County, Missouri and Johnson County, Kansas there are well established linear systems which could serve as a strong foundation for the Metro Green system. In contrast, much of the outer loop of the proposed system is tenuous and fragile. Suburban development easily moves over the stream ways of the plains, submerging natural drainage patterns in pipes. Farmland has proven an ideal site for residential subdivisions and large industrial parks. Little of the potential outer loop has been secured by public ownership. The Metro Green proposal identifies those areas most threatened by current and future development, areas where the green way could provide a valuable buffer between existing and future development. Connections between the two loops could be provided through corridors. Some might follow stream ways, others could follow abandoned rail rights of way. In urban areas, simple sidewalk connections along major thoroughfares could link one loop to the other. Another dimension was added to the proposal with the selection of Phil Lewis, Jr. as an advisor to the project. Long recognized as an important contributor to green way development, Professor Lewis was invited to assist in the design process. At his suggestion, tile inventory of significant historic, cultural, entertainment and commercial locations was analyzed more closely. The proposed green way system winds through a variety of landscapes, both cultural and natural. At Professor Lewis' suggestion, specific locations to allow visitors and residents to learn about Kansas City's unique communities and landscapes were added to the Metro Green proposal. Called "discovery centers," the range of possible sites includes museums, parks, wildlife refuges,

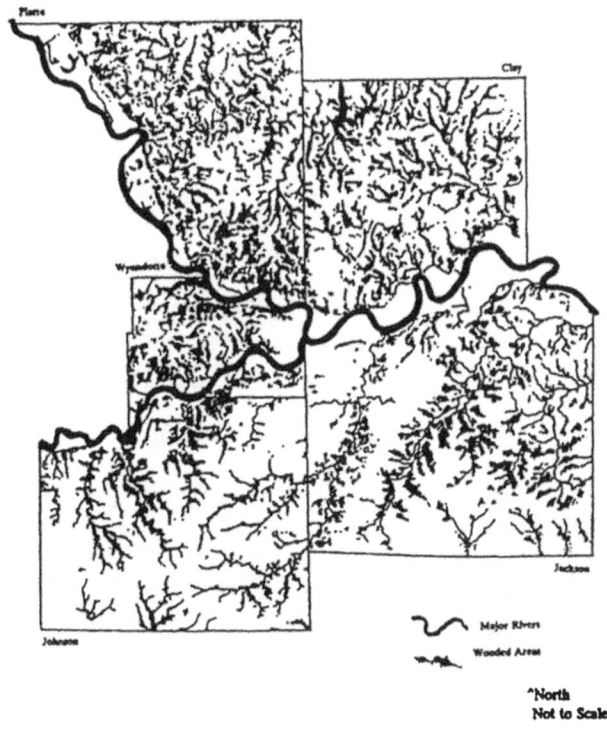

Source: USGS

Figure 5. Woodlands and Stream Corridors in the Kansas City Metropolitan Area

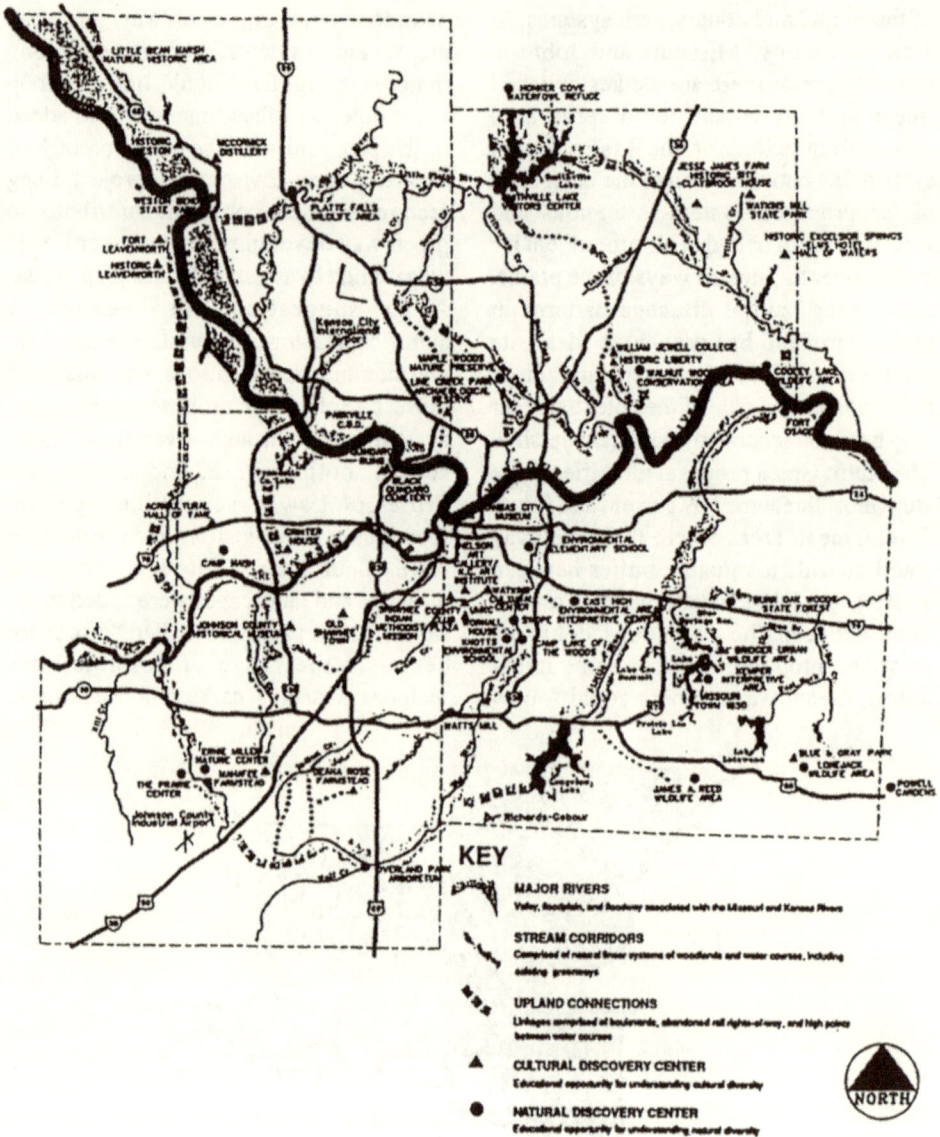

Figure 6. Metro Green Concept Plan

community buildings and commercial recreation sites. Although diverse in character, each would be tied to the Metro Green system by common signage, exhibits and maps of the entire system.

Once revealed, the green way concept was tested and refined. Kansas City area landscape architects met with city staff members, county agencies and local groups to explore the possibilities for the concept in their jurisdictions. After the intensive process of inventory and analysis, refinement and testing, the proposal moved away from site specific recommendations to a very vague map of the proposed system. Assured that the foundation for a comprehensive green way system exists, the project team prepared a proposal for the concept. Maps used for promotion of the idea delineate the potential green way within watershed boundaries. Community names and all but the most significant highways have been omitted, encouraging residents to orient themselves in relation to natural, rather than man made systems. It is hoped that individuals and communities will be inspired to chart the specific path of the system through their part of the city.

THE PROPOSAL

Taken in part, Metro Green represents important recreational and cultural opportunities, many of which already exist. Implementation of any part of the proposal will provide valuable connections between parks and communities. Much of the proposed system builds upon an existing framework of parks and open space with as much of 30 percent of the proposed system already in public ownership. As a whole, the Metro Green proposal could help shape Kansas City in the Twentieth Century in much the same way the 1893 plan shaped the city's early development. This time the linkages to be made are green rather than macadam and the challenge is to contain rather than promote growth.

In a report prepared by ASLA members for presentation to the city, Metro Green is described as crossing

> through the entire range of natural and cultural landscapes to be found in the metropolitan area. It would run parallel to and occasionally be intersected by the main transport routes in the metropolitan area so that it would be highly accessible and well integrated with the roadway network that now exists. It would also link the region's most important museums, nature centers, public gardens and cultural-historical landmarks. In short, it would offer a geographical framework for organizing, experiencing and understanding our natural environment and our cultural heritage. Moreover, Metro Green would also serve as an extraordinary outdoor recreational resource (ASLA, 1991).

The potential benefits include economic, environmental, educational, and recreational improvements. Just as Kessler's plan increased property values at the turn of the century, the success of other green way systems suggests that Metro Green could enhance adjacent property values and, accordingly, property tax revenues (National Park Service, 1990). At the same time, a comprehensive green way system could protect the natural environment and continue Kessler's legacy of sensitive connections between the built and natural environments. While preserving the environment, the green way would provide opportunities for children and adults to learn about ecological relationships within that environment. Development of discovery centers would enrich the educational value of the system. Changing recreational demands call for linear systems to provide people with access to open spaces close to where they live that provide opportunities for walking, jogging and bicycling (President's Commission, 1987). The Metro Green responds to these demands.

The Metro Green proposal stands to benefit from a number of timely circumstances. The centennial celebration of the 1893 Plan for Parks and Boulevards has refocused attention and funding on Kansas City's historic network. Civic pride in the system is growing and expansion of Kessler's legacy is politically popular. As suburban development slows in the 1990s, the Kansas City metropolitan area will have an opportunity to adjust to the new shape and size it acquired during the 1980s. Part of that adjustment will involve planning for parks and open space to serve and buffer newly developed areas. Finally, the nationwide resurgence of interest in greenways should serve the Metro Green proposal well. Recent publications provide technical support and answer questions about implementation, funding, maintenance and other details. The very term greenway is readily recognized by the public and politicians.

PARTNERSHIPS

Metro Green grew out of one specific group, landscape architects, looking for a public service project but the project quickly involved a large number of people and organizations:

- ASLA. Local professional and student members of the American Society of Landscape Architects
- MARC. The regional planning agency for metropolitan Kansas City, Mid-America Regional Council
- Special Interests. Local municipal, county, state and federal agencies with specific interests in the project as well as special interest groups such as the Audubon Society, Sierra Club, and Hiking Association

The effort began with intense effort by landscape architects supported lay governmental agencies and special interest groups. MARC provided important base data, a mailing list, and meeting space and the various agencies and organizations with special interests aided in data collection and review of the proposal. On October 19, 1991, David Warm, Director of MARC, accepted the Metro Green proposal as a gift to the Kansas City area from the American Society of Landscape Architects. On November 18, 1991, the concept will be presented formally to municipal and county agencies in the metropolitan area. The presentation represents a symbolic shift in responsibility. The intent is for the agencies, groups and individuals involved in Implementation of Metro Green to work in a cyclical rather than linear progression. As implementation progresses, responsibilities will change. As anticipated, the individuals, agencies and organizations listed above will be joined by other interested parties. In the next phase, pursuit of the concept will be led by MARC. Through the efforts of MARC, a Metro Green Steering Committee has been named and preliminary funding is in place. The Steering Committee will work with governmental agencies and special interest groups to develop an implementation plan. Landscape architecture professionals and students will provide assistance as an ongoing community service effort.

The process is dependent upon forming and building upon existing partnerships. Initially, landscape architecture students and professionals formed a partnership which allowed extensive inventory and analysis in an academic setting and translation of those ideas by design professionals. This is a simple but often overlooked relationship that offers a wealth of benefits to all involved. The existing Partnerships between MARC and local governments will be essential to implementation of the concept. Local governments look to the Council for information that connects them to the rest of the city. MARC must rely upon the individual jurisdictions to implement specific plans. As the proposal gains momentum, new partnerships will be necessary. Site specific implementation will require private and public sector cooperation. Management and maintenance of the system will most likely require partnerships between governmental agencies and special interest groups.

THE FUTURE FOR METRO GREEN

Even without a cohesive plan, potions of Kansas City will remain green. Floodwaters and rocky slopes will ensure preservation of some open space. But a great deal of open space is in jeopardy. At this point, the proposal for Metro Green remains a concept. Analysis was refined only to the point of identifying major patterns. Maps have been drawn in a way which discourages individual identification of home and property. The next step is for the people who own the homes and property and manage the communities to chart the future of Metro Green.

In 1903, the Olmsted brothers proposed a 40-mile loop for Portland, Oregon as a part of the Lewis and Clark Centennial Exposition. Like the Metro Green proposal, the plan was to link meadows and forest with the parks and boulevards of Portland. It was almost 75 years before significant portion of the loop was completed. Only recently has strong interest spurred implementation of the rest. Today a one hundred and forty mile loop is in progress (Little, 1990). Like Portland's plan, Kansas City's Metro Green is a plan created in celebration of a special event. It is ambitious and far reaching. Early in the process, ASLA members expressed concern that the proposal was too big to be realized. As enthusiasm for the concept grew within the city, those fears turned to questions about how such a large project could be managed. Following George Kessler's advice and the model of cities like Portland, Metro Green has been planned "comprehensively and broadly." The challenge ahead is to implement the proposal for, rather than during, the next century.

Stephanie Rolley, ASLA, AICP, is an Assistant Professor in the Department of Landscape Architecture, Kansas State University. She was responsible for direction of the studio which conducted the inventory and analysis and developed the greenway concept. Questions regarding this project may be addressed to her at KSU, 215 Seaton Hall, Manhattan, KS 66506-2909 or (913) 532-5961.

REFERENCES

American Society of Landscape Architects. (1991). *Metro Green*. Kansas City, MO: American Society of Landscape Architects.

Kansas City Board of Park and Boulevard Commissioners. (1893). *Report of the Board of Park and Boulevard Commissioners*. Kansas City, MO: Hudson-Kimberly Publishing Company.

Little, C. (1990). *Greenways for America*. Baltimore: The John Hopkins University Press.

President's Commission on Americans Outdoors. (1987). *Americans Outdoors: The Legacy, the Challenge*. California: Island Press.

Rivers and Trails Conservation Assistance Program. (1990). *Economic Impacts of Protecting Rivers, Trails, and Greenway Corridors*. Washington, DC: Department of the Interior, National Park Service.

Rolley, S. (Ed.) (1991). *The Kansas City Metropolitan Greenway: A Report by the KSU ASLA CAT Studio*. Manhattan, KS: Kansas State University, Department of Landscape Architecture.

Wilson, W. (1989). *The City Beautiful Movement*. Baltimore: The John Hopkins University Press.

Visual and Environmental Concerns for the Higashi Fujigoko Highway in Japan

Shigeo Sudo

INTRODUCTION

Public interests to visual quality and natural environment related to developments of human society have become very important concerns in Japan. This means that highway constructs have become at the very difficult situation in naturally and visually preserved areas, if the considerations of visual and environmental aspects as well as environmental countermeasures have not been taken into account. "Highway constructions which are gentle to living things" is becoming widely used in Japan.

On the other hand, people who live in developed areas where visual quality and nature have disappeared from the surrounding environment drive out to suburbs every weekend to satisfy their demands for nature. Development of motorization has led people to various nearby sight-seeing areas easily. As a result, traffic jams are common on highways in sight-seeing areas in Japan, especially in touring seasons.

The Higashi Fujigoko Highway passing through at the foot of Mt. Fuji and in the area of the Fuji Hakone Izu National Park, which is one of the tourist meccas in Japan close to the Tokyo district, was planned to dissolve traffic jams while maintaining the visual quality and natural environment of the area. Investigations were conducted to preserve the visual and natural resources of the corridor. This paper documents the results of investigations and the project plan of the visual and environmental countermeasures related to the Higashi Fujigoko Highway (Figure 1).

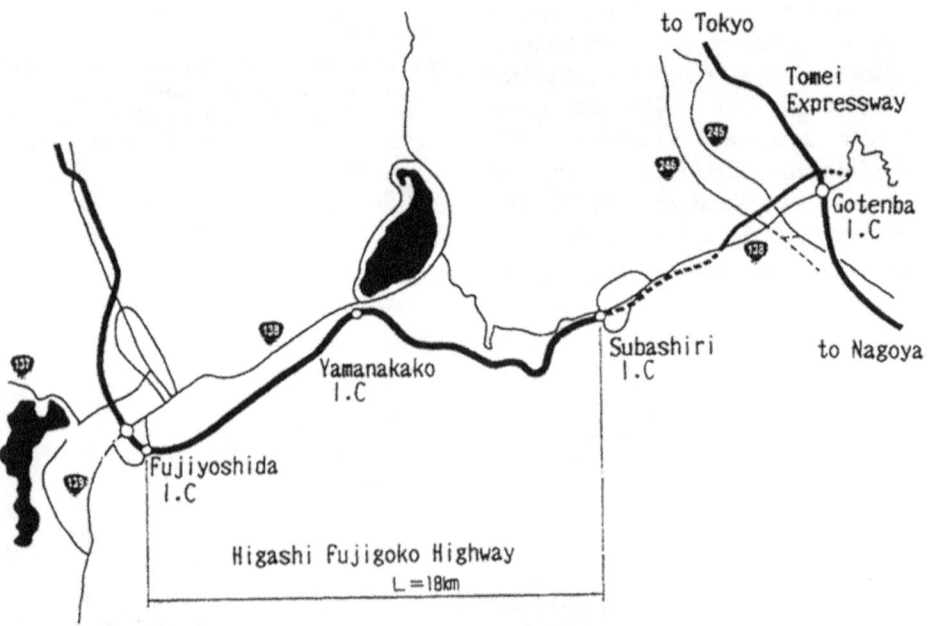

Figure 1. Route map of the Higashi Fujigoko Highway.

Photo 1. Mt. Fuji as veiwed from the Higashi Fujigoko Highway.

INVESTIGATIONS FOR PRESERVING VISUAL QUALITY AND NATURAL ENVIRONMENT

Investigations were conducted to ensure the preservation of the important visual quality and natural environment of the corridor near Mt. Fuji. The objectives of the research were to clarify the visual and natural qualities of the area and to analyze the present situations of existing vegetation, wildlife, soil, and visual landscape elements. A visual landscape analysis was conducted to obtain countermeasures for the destruction of the visual quality of the area—which is one of the most representative sceneries in Japan—and to establish visual landscapes for driving.

Environmental investigations were organized by biosphere, soil, and visual landscape elements. The results of investigations were also reflected in the reuse of

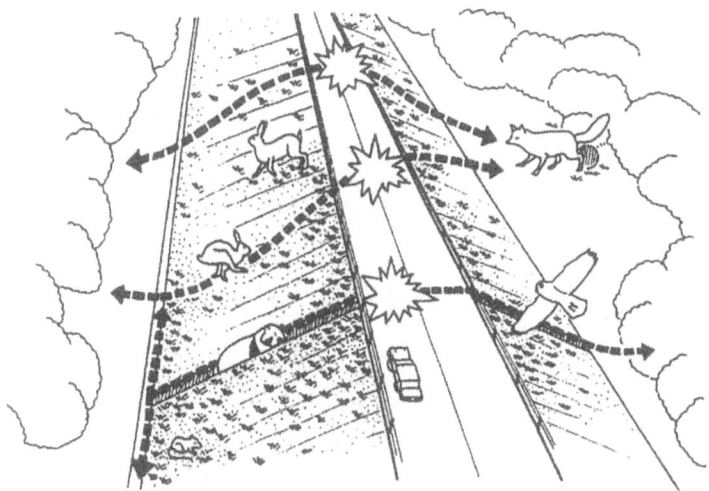

Figure 2. Roadkill from crossing the corridor.

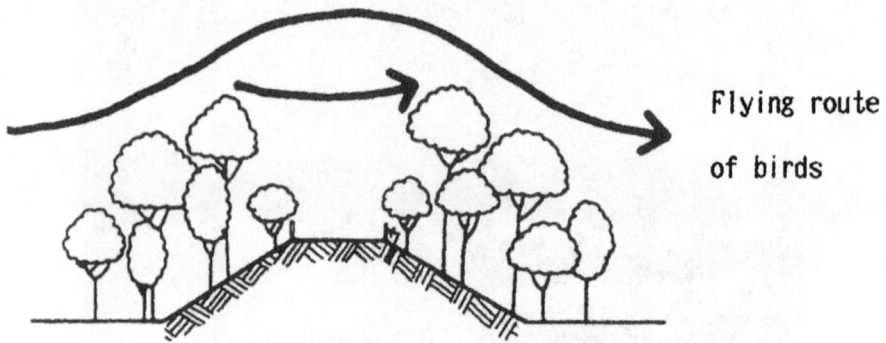

Figure 3. Tall tree planting near the roadway.

top soil for embankments, in the set of culvert boxes for wildlife pass, in bridge design, and in planting design.

Planting design was one of the most important countermeasures to recover vegetation on the destroyed area and to preserve the visual quality (Photo 1).

ENVIRONMENTAL INVESTIGATIONS AND SOME COUNTERMEASURES

Not only animals and plants, but microbes and other things live together symbiotically in soil. Once one of the relationships of the biosphere is destroyed, the balance of the living things which has been kept for a long time will be broken.

In general, nature has its own restorative potential; however, there might be a limitation of the restoration. For example, it is critical in high mountainous regions, serious climate zones, and so on.

Investigations of the biosphere of the corridor were conducted to obtain the biological information and to assess the critical impacts on the biosphere from the highway.

Investigations of Vegetation

Investigations of vegetation were conducted by vegetation group surveys and constitution surveys of species in different areas of natural environment of the corridor. Results of the investigations

Photo 2.
50 cm thickness for topsoil reuse.

Photo 3.
Reusing the topsoil on the embankments.

reveal the important vegetation groups to be preserved in the corridor and pointed out the species to be planted for the planting plan. Several groups of vegetation types, such as Japanese red pine forests, oak tree forests, Japanese beech forests, and so on were listed as preserved vegetation.

Investigations of Wildlife and Birds

Investigations of wildlife and birds were conducted with existing data collection surveys, hearing surveys, field sigh surveys, and a roadside census. As a result, there were no special wildlife and birds which need specific preservation countermeasures in the area of the corridor. However, the results of the investigations revealed the important areas where wildlife and birds expectantly cross the corridor.

It was considered that planting as near the roadway as possible is important in lessening the open space of the corridor (Figure 2). Planting tall trees near the roadway is expected to enable birds to cross the roadway (Figure 3). Planting bushes near culvert boxes is also expected to enable wildlife to use the culvert boxes as wildlife passes.

Photo 4.
The scenery from the viewing point after construction.

Photo 5.
The scenery of
Mt. Fuji at the
Hashigahara segment.

Investigation of Insects

Investigations of insect life were conducted to obtain the change of the environment after the highway construction. If the numbers of specific insects increase after the highway construction. It was pointed out that the reuse of the topsoil and planting native vegetation would lessen the environmental impact of the corridor.

SOIL INVESTIGATION AND SOME COUNTERMEASURES

An investigation of soil was conducted to clarify the condition of the soil in the corridor and to examine the possibility of topsoil reuse. Topsoil reuse, which is one of the most important countermeasures for biosphere preservation, had been done in many places. However, a big project of topsoil reuse was conducted in the construction of the Nikko-Utsunomiya Highway in 1978. Follow-up investigations conducted from 1981 to 1982 revealed that the environmental impacts to the biosphere by the highway construction were very light. Continuous follow-up surveys showed that the growth of the vegetation on the highway was improving and the visual landscape was becoming compatible with the surrounding landscape. Surveys also showed the effectiveness of the utilization of the topsoil which is useful for the planting base and the high-level preservation of the natural environment.

Investigation of the soil was conducted to obtain data of soil cross, physical quality, chemical quality, and soil thickness of the corridor. The biggest problem of topsoil reuse is how to store the mass of topsoil in the corridor. Stock yards of topsoil in the adjacent areas near the corridor will negatively affect the natural environment. In this case, future construction yards were used as stock yards for the topsoil. Stored topsoil reused on the embankments is 50 centimeters in thickness.

VISUAL LANDSCAPE INVESTIGATIONS AND SOME COUNTERMEASURES

Mt. Fuji is the highest mountain in Japan. The landscape which includes Mt. Fuji is one of the most representative sceneries in Japan. The Japanese people love Mt. Fuji and have for a long time.

Many mountains which have the name "Fuji" exist in Japan. Fugaku-sanjurokkei, a set of wood prints of 36 scenes of Mt.

Fuji, printed in the 19th century, says that the people of that time admired Mt. Fuji.

Investigations of visual landscape were conducted to prevent the visual intrusion of the highway into the scenery of the area and to produce fine driving landscapes. Field surveys concerning the highway appearances in the visual landscape along the planned corridor were conducted at 17 points which were documented in the environmental impact assessment report. The contents of the surveys included photographic analysis, measurement of distances from viewing points to the roadway, vegetation analysis, and analysis of planned road structures and other visual elements.

Four points were reported as extremely high visual concerns. Three of these points are visually impacted areas where the roadway passes through the middle scenery zone. Generally, a highway alignment is visually concerned with the middle scenery zone, which is normally defined as the area apart from 1000 to 2000 meters from a roadway to a viewing point. It is important that a highway alignment should be visually compatible with the background scenery. The fourth point is where a bridge was constructed near the scenery zone. In this case, bridge abutments were set back in order to hide them from the viewing point (Photo 4).

It was anticipated that the visual landscape for drives was remarkable scenery because of the open views with grass. In addition, the visual landscape of this area is considered the best scenery with Mt. Fuji along the corridor. Planting tall trees was eliminated and guard cables were used only on the Nashigahara segment of this roadway to take advantage of the excellent scenery (Photo 5).

PLANTING DESIGN

Based on the investigation of the visual resources and vegetation, 3 types of vegetative landscape, representative of Japanese pine forest landscape, deciduous forest landscape, and pine forest landscape, were categorized.

Various species of native vegetation were planted on the embankments and near the roadway to harmonize the highway with the landscape. Investigations were also conducted to identify species and planting density. Basic concepts of the planting design include establishment of previous vegetation as much as possible and creation of the roadway's scenic beauty harmo-

Photo 6. Planting near the roadway.

Photo 7. The harmonized roadway with the visual landscape.

nizing with the visual landscape of the area.

1. Planting should be done at all construction sites.
2. Existing vegetation should be used as much as possible.
3. Planting should be done near the roadway as much as possible, considering the clearance limit to ease crossing roadway for birds.
4. Planting plans should be designed with mixed varieties of vegetation.
5. Planting plans should also be done by compound storied forests and be compatible with the surrounding vegetation.
6. Planting density should be determined based on the density of the existing forests.

These basic considerations were totally applied for the detailed planting design not only for the landscaping of the highway, but also for the recovery of nature on the construction sites (Photos 6 and 7).

CONCLUSION

Follow-up investigations reveal the recovery of the vegetation on the embankments becoming the habitat of small wildlife. These investigations also showed the utilization of culvert boxes for the wildlife passes. The Higashi Fujigoko Highway has gradually harmonized with the visual landscape of the surrounding area by the planted vegetation. Visual and environmental considerations for this highway were supported by the follow-up investigations. Consideration of visual quality and natural environment are vital to preserve natural landscapes and to harmonize highways with surrounding sceneries as well as to create new roadway landscapes for drivers.

Shigeo Sudo is a member of the Japan Highway Landscape Association and the Road Facility Section of the Tokyo First Construction Bureau of the Japan Highway Public Corporation, Tokyo.

Concept Plan for the Highlands Scenic Tour
Micheal L. O'Brien, William E. Shepherd, Sarah Duncan

The Highlands Scenic Tour is a recent addition to the National Forest Service Scenic Byway Program. The tour provides motorists contact with an area of exceptional scenic beauty, abundant historical interest and diverse examples of multiple use forest management. The tour will be an important component in the recreational development of a region rich in natural resources. The tour is significant as an example of the potential for expanding recreational development in the National Forests. The concept plan is noteworthy for its development process and its design proposals.

The purpose of the National Forest Service Scenic Byway Program is to draw attention to outstanding scenery on National Forest lands and to provide opportunities For the public to view well managed and changing forest landscapes. The tour is the first scenic byway designated in the George Washington, and the second Forest byway designated in Virginia after one in the Jefferson National Forest. The concept plan is an example of the opportunity for partnerships in the National Forest projects.

The Concept Plan for the Highlands Scenic Tour was developed by members of the Landscape Architecture Department of Virginia Tech. The plan was funded through a Challenge Cost-Share Agreement entered into by the U.S. Forest Service and The Community Design Assistance Center, College of Architecture and Urban Studies, Virginia Polytechnic Institute and State University. The center is a public service once of the College that provides assistance with physical planning and design to Virginia localities. Tulle center provides faculty and students of the college with the opportunity to participate in community development.

The route follows a 20-mile loop located just off of Interstate 64 in Alleghany and Rockbridge counties making it easily accessible to local, regional and interstate visitors. The route is composed of segments with varied and distinct characters that have abundant scenic and recreational values.

One segment of paved two-lane road follows a deep forested valley along native trout streams. The remains of a pre-civil war iron ore mining community, mines, railroad grades and bridges, and building foundations are evident throughout the valley. This segment is bordered to the west by the Rich Hole Wilderness area. Another segment is a gravel forest service road that climbs the ridge of North Mount airs. The road reveals a sequence of vistas culminating in one of the finest overlooks from the Alleghenies to the Shenandoah Valley and the Blue Ridge. Along the ridge are sandstone outcrops and cliffs and many varieties of flowering shrubs. The third distinct segment of the road is the actual carriage road used by early settlers to cross the mountain. This narrow and windy road descends through rich cove forests. The loop has various examples of timber and wildlife management.

The planning process combined a detailed resource inventory and logging of road characteristics with a synthetic overview of the site in the field to elicit the development concepts. The Plan's proposals included visual management guidelines, an interpretive program, facility developments, roadway improvements and implementation strategies. The main site development proposed is the Campbell

Fields visitor center located near the site of the former mining community, and houses the historical interpretation program. An innovative management demonstration area is proposed along the North Mountain road segment. In the North Mountain Management Demonstration Area new ways of integrating recreation, wildlife, and timber values would be explored as research into sustainable ecosystem management. Features of the development would include the creation of grassy balds for wildlife and scenic enhancement, an observation platform, cove hardwood preserves and uneven-age timber management.

Three Pennsylvania Linear Parks

INTRODUCTION

The following three papers focus intently on two Pennsylvania State Heritage Park efforts and one National Park Service project. All are linear parks and all are intent on developing multiple resources within their boundaries. Our mutual goal in pulling the three projects into a single session was to highlight the work being done in Pennsylvania and to then use the larger D&L project to provide some perspective on the whole heritage development movement currently emerging in the United States.

Thanks to a network of support from Congress, State government and local planning agencies, the state of Pennsylvania is in the midst of a major exploration of linear heritage park development. Drawing on historic sites within thematic regions or corridors and strengthening the mix with natural and recreational interest, the Pennsylvania program builds toward economic development through both increased tourism and increased local awareness and organization. At present, at least four different regions are in a feasibility study phase and at least two others are already moving toward a Management Action Plan for their region.

This session brings papers on three of those projects in Pennsylvania to the linear parks conference. The first deals with the National Road, a pre-industrial transportation project built by the federal government starting in 1815 and still containing a remarkable number of surviving structures, villages, even landscapes of early Federal America. The second deals with the region in which oil was first discovered and developed commercially, a "boom town" region of gushers and rampant environmental devastation that is today an appealing recreational area with a remarkable historic base. The third, the Delaware & Lehigh Canal National Heritage Corridor, is an already-designated corridor just beginning its final master planning phase.

The three sites are different in time, in their historic setting, and in the interests of those advocating their recognition. The three presenters are equally varied, coming from historic preservation, cultural geography and the history of American technology. Together, the projects and their presenters offer a remarkable opportunity to discuss a state linear parks process in the early stages of its implementation and to reflect on the lessons learned for the benefit of those that will come after.

The National Road: A Traveller's Landscape

Stephanie Sechrist

Since the advent of the automobile, the face of the country and our vision as a people has changed remarkably. With the growth of our cities and the disappearance of our rural landscapes, fewer and fewer historic roadways retain their historic significance. Changes to our landscape perceived as positive or necessary are oftentimes detrimental to our sense of place and the survival of our historic roadways and rural landscapes.

Historic roadways provide ample opportunities—for recreation, preservation, conservation of natural and scenic areas, and for economic development and cultural tourism. By their nature, historic roadways cross many boundaries and link many jurisdictions and therefore provide opportunities for preservationists, conservationists, and economic development and tourism officials from many places to work together toward a common goal. It is an incredible opportunity as well as a tremendous challenge. Most important, however, is the preservation of whole places, which is paramount to the retention of history and heritage in a region, community or place.

This paper explores a heritage development project in the Commonwealth of Pennsylvania aimed as conserving and interpreting a portion of the National Road, an early nineteenth century interstate road constructed by the federal government to connect the eastern seaboard with the expanding frontier. One of several Pennsylvania State Heritage Park projects, the National Road Heritage Park Feasibility Study has recently ended. This paper includes a brief history of the National Road, then addresses heritage development as a new tool to preserve historic places that combines preservation, economic development and cultural tourism. Lastly, the challenges faced during the initial planning stages of the proposed National Road Heritage Park are identified.

A truly "National" road was conceived of as early as the 1790s, when Albert Gallatin, Secretary of Treasury under Thomas Jefferson spoke of the need for a federally funded road, suggesting that improved transportation would unite the country and maintain political and economic cohesiveness within the new nation. The proposed road would not traverse through untouched terrain, but instead follow well established, but treacherous trails, blazed first by Native Americans and followed by General Braddock and George Washington during the French and Indian War. With growing numbers of settlers, both traveling and settling in Southwestern Pennsylvania and beyond, and increased trade and communication flowing westward, a more permanent and well constructed road was necessary. The 1790 Whiskey Rebellion of Southwestern Pennsylvania, (a rebellion by farmers who were frustrated by the difficulties of reaching eastern markets), had only reaffirmed the need for better and more direct roads. An interstate road would accomplish many feats—it would facilitate communication between the seat of government and the expanding nation, establish a military presence in the West, and open up trade on the vast river basins of the Ohio and Mississippi. Although the Road was approved by Congress in 1806, it was not begun until 1811 and finally completed to Wheeling, West Virginia, its first terminus, in 1818. Instantly, the National Road became one of the busiest routes in America, carrying ideas, pioneers and freight to and from the West.

A distinct culture and way-of-life immediately evolved along the Road almost entirely generated by, and dependent upon, its traffic. Pike towns were quickly established in response to the economic prosperity associated with the National Road, creating a transportation landscape unfamiliar to the region. This flurry of activity continued well into the early 1850s as the Road expanded into Ohio, Indiana and Illinois.

By the mid 1850s, with the completion of the B&O and the Pennsylvania Railroads to Wheeling and Pittsburgh respectively, the Pennsylvania portion of the National Road lapsed into a state of desertion. The railroad carried people and freight with great speed and efficiency, something with which the Road could not compete. The railroad played a significant role in making Southwestern Pennsylvania a worldwide industrial power, but only along those sections of the National Road where coal and steel drove the economy did the Road remain active. The majority of the National Road in Pennsylvania sat quietly reminiscent of its magnificent past.

Then, in the early twentieth century the National Road enjoyed a brief revival as automobile touring became one of America's favorite past times. Patriotism and the erection of nationalistic monuments commemorated civil war veterans, female pioneers, the French and Indian War, and fallen war heroes like General Braddock. This nationalism, along with the invention of the automobile, attracted travelers to the National Road armed with travel guides to the "Main Street of America," path of the first pioneers. The resurgence of activity along the National Road fostered the construction of garages, gas stations, restaurants and motor courts. In 1926 parts of the National Road were incorporated into U.S. Route 40, a transcontinental highway. Gradually the highway became mainly a route of transport and then, in the 1960s and 1970s, the Road was bypassed by interstate highways. Today, as in the late nineteenth century, the National Road is the road less traveled.

The National Road is an exceptional historic roadway that retains a sense of its original grandeur. Ninety miles of the original Road survive in Pennsylvania, sometimes obscured by development but largely evocative of a pre-automobile road and traveler's landscape. The distinct Road-related resources that survive along many stretches of the old Road in Pennsylvania are strong reminders of an era that took center stage in a national theatre. Many physical manifestations of the era still remain on the landscape: the curves and grades of the original route, the taverns and toll houses, the pike towns, and the rural setting all create a larger sense of place - a real setting for a very real historic place. Remarkably, it is the first era of activity along the Road that is most evident, not the later auto-related layer of growth or any subsequent layers of growth along parts of the Road that are meant to be modernizations. The old Road shines thorough leaving an impression, whether conscious or unconscious, on those who live along it and those who travel it.

There is an urgency to understand, to preserve and to interpret the National Road's history and heritage before it, like too many scenic highways, is lost to disrepair, disrespect or destruction. The preservation and interpretation of the Road and the place will be no small task, nor can it be accomplished by one interest group. Likewise, the Road can not, and should not, be made into a museum. The three county region of Pennsylvania through which the Road passes is a living environment, one that evolves and changes as people and their ideas do. The history and heritage of the region should be conserved for its historic significance, as well as for its significance in the lives of those living in the region. Heritage development is a promising vehicle to achieve this goal.

Heritage development is an approach to place that recognizes that the heritage of a region leaves its footprint on the built, living, and natural environment. Many places that still exhibit their heritage (for example a company town that was developed to house workers of a coal company or a pike town that was founded to meet the needs of travelers on the National Road) fail to see it as a positive asset. They do not see its potential as a foundation for their region's future; instead, they see it as something to be replaced with something new, and therefore better. Heritage development replaces the negative stereotype that history is debilitating with a positive self image for a community, one that can be perceived by an outsider.

Both the federal government and select states have begun to recognize the need to retain large areas or places, representative of an idea or a theme, as increasingly the preservation of individual sites or building neglects the larger picture. Towns, buildings, rural landscapes, traditions and life-styles are recognized within a larger context, one more inclusive and interesting to the average citizen.

Heritage development brings together groups and ideas never thought related, all in the name of preservation, economic development and cultural tourism. Cultural tourism is one of the fastest growing segments of the economy which taps into America's desire to see, hear and touch "history." For visitors, a heritage park or a heritage corridor provides a history lesson of a special place but also a place to relax and enjoy the other recreation and entertainment facilities a region has to offer.

Heritage development requires the cooperation of not just preservationists but conservationists, economic development and tourism officials, as well as private citizens. It is an interesting approach that requires a broad vision, community support, and cooperation between public and private organizations. This type of development reaches across political, economic, social and physical boundaries to foster a consensus approach to regional cooperation and development. Since it is a multifaceted goal its benefits are numerous; a sense of community pride, the preservation of important buildings and sites and their physical surroundings, an increase in visitors, and as a result of all this, a boost to the local economy. Obviously, the visitor will benefit, but the real beneficiaries will be the residents, those fortunate enough to live in an area that is proud of itself and its heritage.

Nationally, three heritage corridors have been designated by the federal government and a growing number of states (like New York, Massachusetts and Pennsylvania) are establishing heritage development programs of their own. The Commonwealth of Pennsylvania has developed the Heritage Parks program, a pioneering heritage development initiative to conserve and interpret the state's industrial traditions into the twenty-first century. Established in 1989 at the initiative of the state's Department of Community Affairs (and not the typical State Historic Preservation Office), the program commemorates the industrial heritage of particular regions within the state, with themes ranging from transportation to steel production to textiles.

A Pennsylvania State Heritage Park is not a "park" in the typical sense. Instead it is a distinct place, regionally defined by and underlying historic theme. The thread that ties these areas together is the combination of historic, cultural, natural, and recreational resources. The resultant environment creates an overall character, a sense of place. In the National Road region, the whole place is essentially a historic district ninety miles long, running through the valleys and atop the ridge lines of Southwestern Pennsylvania, and carrying with it nearly two centuries of national significance. This travelers landscape makes a strong case for Heritage Park development.

The State of Pennsylvania, regional residents, county governments, and private organizations and agencies recognize the significance of the National Road, to the state and the nation as well as to local residents. These numerous groups are now working together to incorporate the area into a Heritage Park. Under the Heritage Parks program, not only individual sites are preserved, but also their environs—the pike towns, rural landscapes, and historic buildings that are contiguous with the National Road. It is not just the Road that is significant and worth preserving, but it is the sense of place created by all those things combined.

The National Road Heritage Park Project is one of several Heritage Park projects now underway in varying developmental stages across the state. The first planning stage, a feasibility study, has just concluded. The focus of this early planning phase was to determine the potential for the National Road region to become a successful Heritage Park. The state required that two goals be met at this early planning stage in order for the area to receive Heritage Park designation and proceed on to the Management Action Plan. First, the resources in the region, the physical manifestations of the National Road and the resultant cultural resources, had to be sufficiently complete and compelling. Second, there had to be adequate regional support, cooperation, and coordination among intergovernmental and interagency organizations to develop and manage the Heritage Park regionally.

Meeting these requirements and adhering to the state's sometimes stringent guidelines proved challenging. It was immediately clear that the historic resources, the old taverns, toll houses, and rural landscapes, were reminiscent and strongly suggestive of a different time and place. The presence of the built, as well as the natural environment, was striking especially because it was the earlier phase of development along the Road that survived with such consistency and strength.

Given the regional economic depression, the length of the linear corridor, the many jurisdictions it traverses, and the typical north-south, not east-west, flow of communication, the level of interagency and intergovernmental cooperation was much less resilient. Not since the heyday of the National Road has the basic political and social orientation of the counties and smaller communities along the National Road run east-west, since the railroads and the interstates shifted communication north and south. What did develop during the planning process was a clear consensus among private citizens, largely business leaders along the National Road, who saw the potential of the Heritage Park and were willing to join together and work for it. Fortunately, as the planning process came to a close, the more active participation of governmental officials on the Steering Committee and a commitment from county governments to actively support the project more closely addressed the state's need for strong intergovernmental and interagency cooperation. Not only did the people of the region learn to see the potential of the National Road Heritage Park, but so too did many local governments and private agencies. The real success of this early planning project was the growing communication among citizens, governments and private agencies throughout the *entire* National Road region in Pennsylvania.

Historic roadways are threatened by becoming a thing of the past. However, these linear corridors are essential to our sense of self. It is hard to imagine a place where there is neither open space not scenic views, but if we neglect our environs, we may very well be faced with this reality in years to come. The Pennsylvania State Heritage Parks program and other heritage development initiatives throughout the country have recognized the impact of preserving and interpreting our larger historic landscapes. Whether they take the form of heritage parks, scenic byways or greenways their results are similar—a place where visitors and residents alike can celebrate in the history and heritage of a place, and at the same time take part in the events, activities, and traditions a region has to offer. As a result of this growing interest in heritage development, the mood is looking brighter for the establishment and preservation of our historic roadways.

Stephanie Sechrist completed her BA in Art History and is currently working on her MA in American Civilization with a concentration in Historic Preservation at George Washington University in Washington, D.C. Her work experience includes a term at Preservation Action, the national lobby group, and a thematic warehouse survey project in Northwest for the D.C. Preservation League. She also has experience in manuscripts and special collections and in photographic conservation and exhibition—both while at the University of Delaware. She served as Co-Director of the National Road Feasibility Study. Her BA degree is in Art History from the University of Delaware, 1990.

Heritage Park and Historic Riverway in the Pennsylvania Oil Region

Randy Mason

This paper is about the planning of a linear, regional heritage park in the Oil Region of northwestern Pennsylvania. The building blocks for the planning effort are the region's history as the birthplace of the modern petroleum industry; the well-informed, enthusiastic and organized citizens leading the effort to conserve . . . and develop; and, from a physical planning perspective the region's stream valleys and its urban system. This paper will outline the process as well as the products of establishing the Oil Region State Heritage Park. I'll start by describing what kind of linear park this is proposed to be, and the factors informing that idea (we know there can be many kinds of linear parks). Then I'll talk about the particular, unique resources and opportunities present in the Oil Region and how they might be synthesized into a plan and a set of actions to create this regional park.

What kind of linear park will the Oil Region Heritage Park be? The shortest way to say it is that it will be a regional partnership park, based on industrial history, and designed to incorporate both conservation and economic development goals as well as some others. The planning process is sponsored by the Commonwealth of Pennsylvania's Heritage Parks Program, which provides matched planning grants and some implementation funds to highlight those areas that have a significant industrial history (Pennsylvania as a state is nationally significant in this regard) and have been hit hard by the advent of the postindustrial economy. The program primarily aims to preserve and interpret industrial heritage and develop cultural tourism based on that heritage (this focus on the industrial complements the state's other tourism marketing focus on political and military history, sloganized under the "America Starts Here" banner.)

Pennsylvania Heritage Parks (of which there are nine in different stages of development) are, as I said, partnership parks, designed to foster cooperation among various public, private interest groups and agencies. Partnership parks are contrasted with conventional parks in that they do not require land being brought under public ownership; it is not a piece of real estate with a fence and gates around it, it's better described as a web of commitments and mutual agreements. The state's Heritage Parks Program manual reads: "A Pennsylvania Heritage Park is a process as well as a product." [sic] The efforts made at fostering cooperation and maintaining region-wide dialogues are as important as the implemented plans and parks themselves. Within the overall goals of preserving the state's industrial heritage and improving the quality of life in the communities the Program maintains five explicit goals:
- economic development: the bottom line
- cultural conservation: physical and human (these two are often seen as competing, but these parks bring them together)
- intergovernmental and interagency cooperation: the process framework and the strongest way to build broad support
- education
- recreational development.

For a region to proceed through the multistage planning and implementation process, the local Task Force must document their progress toward meeting these five goals.

The early stages of heritage park planning call for development of an historic theme (based on the industrial history and extant resources) and rough boundaries. The theme is self-evident in the Oil Region! (It can be more problematic in other, more diverse regions, such as the Schuylkill River.) I'd like to focus on the boundaries here because they speak most directly to shape and linearity.

Although it is officially called a heritage park, the geography and history of the Oil Region suggests that it would more appropriately be called a heritage corridor: There is a linear structure that characterizes the planning region stemming directly from industrial history and development of the oil industry along Oil Creek and the Allegheny River. This linear structure is used as the base resource— the spine—for the corridor. Some have called this structure—this pattern—an "historic riverway," a term that capture the industrial historical theme as well as the natural/physical presence and importance of the streams and their valleys.

HISTORY / GEOGRAPHY

Now that the planning process and the heritage park concept have been introduced, let me back up and outline the history and the geography that this whole thing is based upon ... and how the "historic riverway" came to be.

Before 1859, the Oil Region was an inaccessible, sparsely populated region of the Alleghenies. Near Titusville in 1859, oil was recovered by drilling through about 60 feet of rock and "sands." This event permanently changed the region. This discovery of oil and the experience of creating an industry created the region. All the early innovations of technology and management were devised here, from the hardware to John Rockefeller. When word of the oil discovery got out, it set off an enormous boom period. The was a ready market for illumination and lubrication oil, and fortune-seekers came in droves. More people came to the Pennsylvania oil boom of the 1860s, it is claimed, than participated in the California gold rush a decade earlier. Hillsides were cleared and derricks sprouted everywhere. Hay farms became oil farms.

During this period (1859 to the early 1870s) a compact urban system was created to extract, transport, and trade oil. Different small cities performed the different functions of the oil industry and were closely integrated by economic structures as well as by the drainage spine down Oil Creek to the Allegheny River (and from there on to Pittsburgh). From north to south, Titusville (production center), Oil City (corporate, exchange and manufacturing center), Franklin (county and regulatory seat), and Emlenton (small refinery and capitalists town), remain today to tell the story of the early oil industry. Some of the most fascinating and entertaining stories, though, are told by a fifth type of place, which no longer exist, really: the oil boomtown. Although there are many examples, the foremost is Pithole City. Nothing of the this city of 15,000 remains today, except some cellar holes and the small visitor center signifying that it is a state historical site. The place was built and taken down in the space of a few years; when the oil ran out locally, there was no reason to stay and houses were dismantled and taken elsewhere.) The initial ten or fifteen years of industrial and urban development that brought on the boom are the focus of the Heritage Park. The communities created during this period today comprise a remarkably intact region with great potential for interpretation.

Having been educated as a landscape historian and cultural geographer, the most fascinating aspect of all this is the set of relationships between the human histories and the material histories. By this I mean the relationship between the natural resources that enabled the oil industry to grow, the innovators who made things work and made a lot of money, the economic system that was created, and the built environment that was shaped by and for this industry: the mineral itself, the knowledge of stratigraphy and salt well drilling for the initial discovery; the tight steep valleys of the Alleghenies, the innovation of pipelines to bypass teamster transportation, and the building of cities in this rugged, isolated natural landscape. This place has an extraordinary feel because, knowing just a bit about this early history, one can see the historical patterns and relationships present in the contemporary natural and urban landscapes of the region. The small cities of the region, as I said, were functionally different parts of the oil economy, and today the urban form of each reflects this in the mix of buildings, the town's location, the orientation of the grids, and so on. In the towns the only clear vistas are along the river, giving a sense of why the riverway has been so important to this region. There are several refinery complexes remaining in the region, but the more interesting technological, historical resources are the pieces of old (and still used) oil extraction machinery, pipes and tanks strewn about the woods all over the place. This speaks to the continuity of the oil industry over more than a century: although the methods, technology, economy, form, and environmental regulation of the industry have certainly been transformed, the industry survives: a living heritage and an active force in shaping the contemporary landscape.

The pattern established in that initial period of development remains remarkably strong, especially in the built environment and character of the communities and the linkages between places. Although altered by such watershed changes in geography and history and the coming of the railroads in earnest in the 1870s, the decline of the industry regionally after discoveries elsewhere in northern Pennsylvania and later in Texas and Oklahoma, the establishment of the highway system, and postwar urban decline, this historical pattern of the development of the oil region—and the continuing industry itself—is quite apparent today and is one of the region's most valuable and valued resources. This pattern of urban places and stream valleys is such that no one place is a typical oil town, and to really understand this place and the early history, one must visit all the places, rally see the region. This has very positive implications for cultural tourism in the region.

Today, although the postindustrial economy has hit this region very hard, the residents show uncommon determination and resilience, they really care about this place and they strongly identify with the place's oil history as the defining quality of their region . . . oil and oil heritage remain a part of everyday life here (and as much as we have heard this claimed in any number of places, it is truer here than anyplace I've encountered) . . . Quaker State and Pennzoil remain as respected business community presences

OPPORTUNITIES

From analyzing the historic resources and the contemporary resources of the region, and gleaning from the public and from community leaders a sense of their goals, my firm, as planning consultants to the local Heritage Park Task Force, has worked to identify some of the potential opportunities presented by the park.

Regional cooperation and development: there is the opportunity to realize the benefits of joint action and the pooling of resources and expertise; this is a plan to improve the quality of life in the region and all its communities; to raise the level of the lake and all the individual boats with it; the region has already demonstrated that it can effectively cooperate; the heritage park would help establish and reinforce the structures of regional cooperation that will make it easier to expand the scope of cooperative efforts in the future.

Heightened sense of place and community pride: the rallying point of park development and planning is regional history; it will be a primary basis for setting boundaries, establishing linkages between existing resources, building public support and generating revenue through cultural tourism; awareness of local history helps solidify the sense of place beyond that evoked by the physical and interpretive resources and reinforces the pride of citizens in their community and in the larger sense of the region; the education goals implicit in the focus on history are really seen by the broadest band of residents as one of the foremost benefits of the park, in addition to being one of the state's avowed goals; the story of the region's development—the story of oil—will be targeted to multiple audiences: visitors and tourists who come seeking such information; local and regional schoolchildren who are taught local history in the fourth grade, but who might benefit from being taught the history of the region beyond the boundaries of their community; and lastly to all residents of the region (newcomers and old-timers) who often don't realize the great value and excitement in the history of their community and the common bonds the share with surrounding communities.

Recreation and open space: A third opportunity for the Oil Region Heritage Park lies in continuing to develop recreation facilities and open spaces. These kinds of amenities, as we know, are attractions both for visitors and residents. They directly affect the quality of life for local residents (and in so doing also improve the posture of Oil Region communities in ongoing endeavors to attract businesses to locate in the region). Recreation and open space projects can also be designed to reinforce the linear linkages underlying the region's history, thereby providing interpretive opportunities. The Oil Region has been quite successful in creating some of these recreation linkages, in the form of riverside bike trails. A regional rails-to-trails organization is very actively working on expanding the network of trails. Bike tails are a good example to demonstrate how one project, if coordinated under a Heritage Park umbrella, can work toward several goals: a single bike trail can be a recreational project, an interpretive project (with signage to tell the story to users), an economic development project (a direct amenity for communities, a draw for tourism), and a project that fosters and utilizes regional cooperation.

Economic opportunities: cultural tourism; continuing industrial development; downtown revitalization; addressing inconsistencies in housing markets (shrinking cities and dependent, aging populations); opportunity for addressing these problems comprehensively, as related issues, as regional issue, not as separate pieces requiring piecemeal solutions.

LINKAGES

Now, having a sense of the broad range of opportunities that the Oil Region Heritage Park presents, we can ask about physical and programmatic planning linkages to tie together some of these opportunities into a coherent linear structure (that makes sense to residents and tourists intuitively and graphically).

Interpretive linkages: rediscovering the history of the boom years; forging and comprehensible, comprehensive visitor experience (you can't see just one town in the Oil Region and say you've seen a typical oil town; the places here are complementary and different, the region is a whole comprised of distinct communities and linkages) to interpret oil history and present an effective tourism economic development tool (longer stays)

Programmatic linkages: expanded regional dialogue (already established by the HP initiative and other efforts) ... expanded regional entrepreneurship (established by the OC&T Railroad) ... expanded joint marketing efforts ... possible region-wide technical assistance sponsored by ORHP Council.

Natural linkages: focus on the streams themselves: Oil Creek and the Allegheny River: the lifeline of the initial boom, the spine of the region's development (historic riverway) ... what gives the ORHP its linear structure, its intuitive strength, its common sense role in the redevelopment of the region because it enabled the initial industrial development of the region ... indications that the streams are returning to their former prominence: Allegheny designation as National Recreation River, the Oil Creek State Park, interest in water recreation, interest in environmental concerns can't be overlooked.

Many industrial places that emerged in the 19th century along linear river systems, especially in the east in the pre-railroad era, have significant potential for rediscovering their historical and physical/environmental roots. Through heritage planning, some regions are realizing that they can use their historic, natural and human resources to build partnerships and plans for the future and prosperity of the region—and not as single communities in isolation.

Pennsylvania's Oil Region is in the process of rediscovering and redeveloping *its* linear geography—its historic riverway—through planning a regional, linear heritage park. For the Oil Region, at least, it looks like the linear shape is the shape of the future as well as its past.

Randy Mason is a cultural geographer and planner who coordinates the geographic resource surveys at TMA. A graduate of Pennsylvania State University, where he studied with Pierce Lewis, Mason brings a close working knowledge of the physical and cultural geography of Pennsylvania. He taught Regional Geography to undergraduates at Penn State, worked as an Editorial Researcher for *National Geographic* Magazine and the Historical Atlas of the United States (published by the National Geographic), and presented a paper on "A New Cultural Geography" to the Association of American Geographers in 1990. His MS degree is in Cultural Geography from Pennsylvania State University, 1990; his BA is in Geography and English from Bucknell University, 1986.

The Delaware & Lehigh Canal: Heritage Development in Perspective
Whole Places and New Partners in Linear Parks
T. Allan Comp, Ph.D.

Fifteen years ago the historic preservation and recreation agencies of the federal government were merged into a new agency, the Heritage Conservation and Recreation Service. While that decision and its consequences created enough controversy to last the rest of the century, it also created a few real projects that, seen in some perspective, proved to be remarkable in their anticipation of future trends. One of those projects was a linear park planning project, focused on the historic preservation, recreation and economic revitalization potentials of the Lehigh Canal, an early 19th-century transportation canal in eastern Pennsylvania. A summer-long study concluded there was great potential, resource inventories and economic revitalization case studies were completed, local agency heads and politicians announced their support. Just as effective momentum for the project began to build, Ronald Reagan took over the White House, HCRS was merged into the National Park Service, and federal budgets were slashed. The project report and its list of supporters went to the file for lost hopes, but its content never really disappeared from the agendas of many involved.

Today, thanks largely to cooperation between Congressional delegations and local interests, the Lehigh Canal is part of the Delaware & Lehigh National Heritage Corridor, one of three National Heritage Corridors in the United States. The project is (rather reluctantly) directed by the National Park Service, which received a specific line-item appropriation (essentially an order from Congress) to plan the Corridor. While it is essentially a top-down planning effort, there is a conscious effort to inform and enlist the local interest groups that once formed the Lehigh Canal project coalition as well as others along the Delaware Canal and those to the north where only rails could carry the Anthracite coal that created the need for the transportation system in the first place. Primary activists are those seeking better land use protection in Bucks County and advocates of tourism and economic development along the Lehigh and further north. They form an odd mix of history buffs, avid recreationists and environmentalists, community and economic development agencies, tourism advocates, and representatives from areas with economies so devastated that history may be one of their most marketable commodities.

Perhaps even more revealing, throughout the country there are increasing numbers of disparate (sometimes even desperate) attempts to create something bigger than an historic district, braver than a conservationist's defensive posture, stronger than most advocates current ties to constituents, and directly linked to Congressional interests. These heritage development efforts come under an infinite variety of titles and they have existed in some form for many years, but they all seem to share a common frustration with a traditional narrow definition of place and an equally narrow definition of constituent. National heritage corridors, state heritage parks, national rivers, cultural tourism projects, historic reserves, national recreation areas, national scenic areas, national rivers and trails, historic highways, and several other kinds of places are being developed in every part of the country. They are trying hard, as part of their program, to incorporate a developmental and expansive approach to the sense of whole place and whole people, to break one old and worn intellectual tradition in both recreation and historic preservation and replace it with a larger vision of both strategy and tactics. These heritage development areas challenge us with the opportunity to rethink traditional approaches and partners—indeed, they demand it if recreation, conservation and historic preservation interests are going to play more than defense in this game. Even better, these regional approaches offer an opportunity to reassert an old role as advocate, to get back in front of the parade and lead an expanded and expanding constituency.

Although there are only three federally designated and formally titled National Heritage Corridors at present, there are many earlier examples with different names, and the number of new areas under development is in the hundreds. Even before Lowell National Historic Park became the model for heritage tourism and development, Golden Gate National Recreation Area and Gateway National Recreation Area in New York City included large numbers of historic resources within their boundaries and were created to encourage tourism, recreation, and some form of economic development. Indeed, the National Park Service manages more National Recreation Areas than it does formal National Parks and they may rival parks for the total number of historic resources within their boundaries as well. Other areas, like Ebey's Landing National Historic Reserve in Washington state and the Pinelands in New Jersey were essentially growth management efforts within areas remarkable for their comfortable mix of natural, scenic, recreational, and historic resources. Using this exact same mix of resources and the same desire for economic development and growth management, the Illinois-Michigan National Heritage Corridor (the nation's first) started with a practical sense of the possible and a small plan of what could happen in just one town along the canal. Today it continues that leadership, developing ever more expansive constituents for Corridor development efforts, bringing in groups and interests once overlooked or passed by, and maintaining its practical sense of the possible.

The processes that are creating this recent surge in interest in heritage development are neither complex nor hard to find. For at least the last ten years if not forever, Congress has been interested in finding ways to put good projects in its own districts. If defense plants and giant highways loose favor, then something else needs to take its place. At the same time, issues like cultural landscapes, local involvement, growing recreational interests, tourism and economic development, and public history all created fertile ground for Congressional seed. Because no one in Congress is interested in essentially defensive and particularist thinking (at least not in public), the more expansive and inclusive were these projects, the more they dealt with the whole place and all the interests in it, the more strongly they were supported.

To gain the wide base of support that Congress requires to do almost anything, the people developing these heritage projects turned to every possible constituency. People trying to raise interest in an old highway or canal discovered there were other forms of conservationists interested in outdoor recreation along on in that same historic site. In other places, bicycle trail advocates teamed up with river and nature groups and then discovered their project was actually located in an historic transportation corridor, a good stroke that brought in a few more advocates and gave the whole enterprise a certain cachet at least. More important, both the historic and the recreation advocates discovered their numbers could create an economic presence in a place and economic development and tourism quickly became the byword of most, if not all, of the heritage development regions.

The point of all this was not to somehow hoodwink an unsuspecting Congressional committee, it was to build a wide base of support directly linked to the area of the project and to assure some economic benefit would accrue to the expenditure of federal dollars. Whatever the organizers choose to call the area—heritage park, national river or trail, historic highway, or recreation area, they made sure the local residents were behind the effort and would benefit from it.

Advocates wisely found every possible source of support for each project, whether it be prairie grass conservationists, bed and breakfast developers, environmental hardliners, history buffs, outdoor recreationists, or kids that just wanted to fish. What they did, even if unknowingly, was to demand a new definition of historic place—vastly larger and more encompassing than the traditional sites, buildings, and districts — and an equally new definition of recreation interests—larger and comfortably inclusive. And this broad constituency-building and place-definition is working, time after time, place after place, no matter what the name of the place or its essential historic characteristic. When it attracted the citizen support, it worked.

The next step in this process was to find an agency within the federal government that could be given money in a line item within the budget and told to spend it on a particular project. The agency most often selected has been the National Park Service, in part because there is a long tradition of doing so, in part because of its park planning, recreation, and historic preservation offices, and in part because of its ease of access and direction within the Interior budget. In the past, the NPS assumed a strong leadership role (creating the partnership with state recreation and historic preservation offices that remains a model today), but lately that leadership role is being forced on the NPS by Congress and its constituents. Indeed, one might argue that virtually all of the new planning and development directions taken by the National Park Service in the last twenty years were initially forced on the Park Service by Congress, and often to the detriment of the core Park Service mission. While support for park maintenance and other essentially boring budget areas languished, support for line-item Park Service projects and technical assistance efforts in these new heritage places throughout the United States increased significantly.

There are other logical reasons for Congressional preference for the National Park Service over other possible agencies. The Park Service is big, it has a large office in the Denver Service Center filled with the necessary kinds of expertise to plan and develop the first steps of these heritage development projects and that office works on soft project dollars: it is the willing (sometimes anxious) beneficiary of Congressional interest in new things to plan and assist. Most important, the National Park Service is generally perceived in Congress and in these new places as user-friendly. They are the good guys doing good things with the People's money and there is no safer way to spend public funds, at least most of the time. The best advantage for us in the recreation and historic preservation worlds is that most of this money for new places passes through the hands of the agency most responsible for historic preservation, archeology, recreation, rivers and trails, and all the other things residing in what was once the Heritage Conservation and Recreation Service and are now within the Cultural Resources offices of the NPS. We—the recreation and historic preservation interests— are literally standing in the doorway with heritage development opportunities running right over us. We need only to catch up with the process, both intellectually and administratively.

This heritage development pattern of linkage among strong constituents, active Congressional leaders, the National Park Service, and the heritage offices within the Park Service creates some interesting and promising relationships that harken back to an earlier grassroots era. Because the Park Service sees its core mission as far different from the needs of these new heritage places, it tends to advocate temporary, technical assistance efforts to aid these places over any long-term commitment. There are exceptions like West Virginia, where a powerful Senator is creating a permanent need for NPS personnel throughout the state, but only a very few states will ever enjoy that kind of committee leadership. Because most of Congress no longer enjoys an unfettered budget, this interest in assistance, in developing large places for multiple enjoyments without buying the whole thing and calling it a park, is reinforced. The result is an approach that does what recreation and historic preservation interests started out with—an emphasis on temporary governmental assistance to local groups who must then carry the burden and do the work themselves.

The multiplicity of support groups required to make these heritage places possible also works against any particular aspect of a plan that would create two clear sides to an issue. If purchasing land creates tension in the assembled supporters, restraint is often self-imposed by the group to assure their success—deals are made, and the process moves forward. Indeed, because of the inclusive interests of these projects, they more often than not depend wholly on consensus planning, on non-directive but persistent leadership, and on independent judgement (NPS or consultants) to surface and assist in resolving the harder or more divisive issues. It consistently appears that the deep human connections between these places and their supporters quickly become the perspective used to unite, to overarch the smaller differences. It is an old and common technique to use the ties to place as a way to build a larger sense of community interest in that same place, but it is one recreation and historic preservation fail to use expansively. Too often, the focus is on protection, on "keeping the heritage in heritage park," while others are building constituents with our best agenda.

One brief illustration of this community and constituency-building aspect of heritage development can be drawn from the Delaware & Lehigh National Heritage Corridor. The effort is being coordinated by the Delaware & Lehigh National Heritage Corridor Commission—twenty-one people who represent towns, counties, historical, recreation, business and environmental interests in the region, as well as the heads of several key state agencies and the National Park Service. The Commission's charge is to draft the plan that will shape the partnerships that will establish and maintain the Corridor. The plan will encourage preservation of important historic buildings, structures, and cultural landscapes—including scenic vistas and areas of natural beauty. A second goal is to make the important heritage of the region come alive through exhibits, tours, signage and other interpretive and educational programs. A third goal is to extend and enhance recreational opportunities for residents and visitors alike, particularly a Corridor-long trail. Equally important, the plan is intended to bring economic opportunity to the Corridor and its communities.

Besides coordinating the plan, the Corridor Commission is providing assistance to a number of local efforts that advance the overall goal. Although the planning process won't be finished until the summer of 1992, the tourist promotion agencies in Bucks County, the Lehigh Valley, and the Poconos, worked with the National Park Service and produced 200,000 copies of a guide to the area and its heritage attractions. Three environmental groups—the Nature Conservancy, the Wildlands Conservancy, and the Bucks County Conservancy—examined the entire Corridor to identify recreational opportunities, significant ecological areas, and important greenspaces and scenic vistas. Penn State University researchers identified cultural landscapes and the Hugh Moore historical Park and Museums along with the Pennsylvania Historical and Museums Commission identified historic resources. The Pennsylvania Heritage Affairs Commission is studying the dozens of ethnic groups in the region, assessing the imprint of their cultures on the region.

On the more developmental side, the Lehigh River Foundation, a consortium of business leaders formed to support the Corridor, had commissioned a film of the Lehigh Valley portion of the Corridor, a professor at Muhlenburg College is making a photographic study of the Corridor, and Wilkes University is planning a symposium on the history of the Corridor. Leadership Lehigh Valley, a joint venture of three area Chambers of Commerce, studied the industrial history and current condition of the area and the feasibility of organizing a corps of college-age Rangers to guide visitors at various points in the Corridor. Following a series of public workshops, the Commission announced eight "Directions" for the Corridor planning effort that exemplify the diversity of their interests. They are:

- Complete a continuous 150-mile bike-hike trail
- Restore or stabilize canal towpaths and structures
- Create curricula on local cultural and natural history
- Establish a program for cultural and natural history
- Improve visual and recreational access to canals and rivers
- Develop cultural tourism opportunities
- Market and rehabilitate underused historic sites
- Protect scenic areas, scenic roads, and vistas

The pattern here is as old as recreation

and historic preservation, but it's new as well. Citizen interest, local political interest, even some willing agency assistance are not remarkable. On the other hand, multiple-county cooperation, interagency support among federal entities, political support from state and federal elected officials, and strong interest from recreation and conservation groups all centered on a complex historic site stretching from the Delaware Bay to the anthracite coal fields are remarkable. The Delaware & Lehigh; National heritage Corridor is being transformed into a long thread weaving together disparate interests, creating a strong sense of whole place, and enabling those living within it to work cooperatively, effectively, and with great success. It is a project vastly larger than the standard historic district, certainly braver than any of the single agencies or individuals whose cooperation made it happen, and it linked directly to the strongest political offices in the region. The National Park Service provides only technical and managerial expertise and works with the Commission to achieve the goals of the planning process. Today, improved recreational use, increased tourism and new opportunities for economic development all animate the D&L Corridor, bringing continued support from a broad spectrum of constituents for ongoing efforts.

A recent survey of heritage development efforts by Preservation Action (the national grassroots lobby group) found nearly one hundred groups at one stage or another of creating their own Delaware & Lehigh or I&M Canal heritage corridor. Typically, state recreation or historic preservation offices and similar advocates are seldom in the lead. Instead, tourism, community development, economic development, or independent conservancies and other non-profits are in the lead, gaining new constituents, learning new perspectives and developing the political ties essential to success. This early failure to fully realize the new opportunities within heritage development seems a tragic loss. These heritage development projects are large and will eventually include vast numbers of park and historic resources within a much more supportive environment—need we ask more? These same heritage development projects will garner strong and effective constituent support because they must do so to succeed—do we require a formal invitation to participate in this expansive constituency support?

One of the fascinating things about these large and complex projects is the range of interests and perspectives that can be brought to bear in developing support. The process offers the opportunity to learn from environmentalists what they care about and why—as well as what it is they do that gets them millions of members; to learn from recreational bicyclists that they actually do care about what they ride through and would, if offered the opportunity, be refreshed by an interpretative sign that helped them understand the whole environment; to learn from the tourism types just what really makes a small market work and from the economic development types just what it takes to put out an effective welcome mat—both vital perspectives if our small towns are to survive; and to learn from ourselves just how far we really can stretch, how many new inputs we can absorb, how many new tricks we can still teach this old dog. Heritage development also offers us the opportunity to teach, to communicate the real value of ties between ourselves and our pasts and to demonstrate the vitality of recreation, landscapes and historic places in contemporary life. It's been fifteen years since there was much being done by the federal government for recreation or historic preservation and its clear that the process is still moving only one project at a time, but it is moving. The growing strength and numbers of these heritage development projects promises continued development—and the continued opportunity to better shape just what these projects ought to be. This inexorable journey into heritage development could promise a more vital intellectual content and context, as well as a deeper connection between the resources we value, ourselves, and those around us—it depends largely on our ability to participate usefully and effectively.

T. Allan Comp is an historian working as Senior Associate with Means and Associates, a planning and heritage development firm. He resides in Washington, D.C. Dr. Comp previously served as Senior Historian for the Historic American Engineering Record, where he developed and directed a series of HCRS rehabilitation planning studies including Lockport, Illinois; and as Chief of the Cultural Resources Division in the Pacific Northwest, where he directed the Columbia River Scenic Highway project and a series of vernacular landscape studies of Ebey's Landing. He currently serves as Project Director for the Management Action Plan for the Delaware & Lehigh National Heritage Corridor and for several other heritage park and historic site interpretive and development projects in the United States, Poland, and Russia.

Development of a State Roadside Vegetation Management Plan in Wisconsin

Paul E. Skidmore and Bruce F. Woods

PREFACE

This paper is excerpted in large part from the "Roadside Vegetation Management Policy" that was developed by the Office of Highway Maintenance of the Wisconsin Department of Transportation. The "Roadside Vegetation Management Policy" was produced by the Roadside Vegetation Management Committee under the direction of Ted Stephenson, P.E., the State Maintenance Engineer for Highways. The authors of this paper have selected and edited appropriate sections of the Policy to present the proposed comprehensive plan to manage the vegetation along Wisconsin's roadsides. Currently, vegetation inventories are being conducted, and vegetation management plans are being prepared. As the implementation of the "Roadside vegetation Management Policy" progresses, the various elements of the overall policy will be evaluated and modified as necessary.

ABSTRACT

In 1990 the Wisconsin Department of Transportation (WiDOT) developed the State Roadside Vegetation Management Policy for Wisconsin. WiDOT developed this policy through discussions with the Roadside Vegetation Management Committee, which included state end county highway commissioners, wildlife and vegetation experts, the Wisconsin State Patrol, state highway maintenance personnel, landscape architectural consultants and concerned citizens.

The Roadside Vegetation Management Policy establishes vegetation management priorities along Wisconsin roadsides. Other policies and plans address, or will address other policy issues related to highway roadsides.

The Roadside Vegetation Management Policy identifies seven major components that are central to a comprehensive and effective policy on roadside vegetation management. These components are: 1) the highway system, 2) vegetation, 3) aesthetics, 4) wildlife, 5) vegetation management, 6) vegetation inventory, and 7) vegetation management plans.

The highway system component identifies the roadside and its associated vegetation as an integral part of the highway system. The entire highway systems includes roadways, roadsides, structures (bridges), and roadside facilities (rest areas, weigh stations, information centers, etc.).

The vegetation component identifies the types of vegetation associated with Wisconsin roadsides. This vegetation includes: trees, shrubs, turf, and ground cover. Vegetation can be indigenous or foreign, and it also can be natural or restored.

The aesthetics component identifies the appropriate visual character of Wisconsin roadsides. Roadsides should complement what lies beyond the edge of the right-of-way, and should not compete with Wisconsin's visual character. Since the roadside is only a small part of the motorist's field of view, it should not detract from the whole viewshed.

The wildlife component identifies the appropriate role of wildlife in the Wisconsin roadside. Reasonable effort should be made to preserve existing habitat on roadsides. Roadsides should be managed to provide an environment suitable for wildlife to live and reproduce, provided that motorist safety is not jeopardized by doing so.

The vegetation management component identifies appropriate alternative methods of managing roadside vegetation. These vegetation management methods include mowing and cutting, pesticide application, burning, and integrated pest management.

The vegetation inventory component identifies alternate methods of locating and classifying roadside vegetation. Elements of the vegetation inventory include: vegetation species, location, size, density, roadside vegetation type, native plant community remnants, presence of rare or endangered species, and aesthetic values.

The vegetation management plan component identifies the recommended plan for inventorying, managing, and monitoring Wisconsin roadside vegetation. The plan initially calls for pilot vegetation inventories in each of the eight WiDOT highway districts while management policies and guidelines are being developed. The plan then calls for a six year statewide vegetation inventory, and the implementation of appropriate vegetation management techniques.

After the Wisconsin State Roadside Vegetation Management Policy was adopted by WiDOT in 1991, two additional documents were developed to put the policy to use. From the policy, an administrative rule was developed. This rule provides authority to WiDOT to implement the policy in the state. From the administrative rule a roadside maintenance manual was developed. This document contains the guidelines and mechanisms by which the policy will be implemented in the field. Currently, WiDOT is conducting pilot vegetation inventories, and preparing specific elements of the Roadside Vegetation Management Plan.

INTRODUCTION

Roadsides are an integral part of the highway system. They protect the highway facility itself, and promote highway safety by providing a recovery area for errant motor vehicles.

Roadsides comprise the area from the pavement shoulder to the property (right-of-way) edge. In Wisconsin, there are about 150,000 acres of roadsides. Three major policy areas apply to Wisconsin's roadsides. They are:

1. vegetation
2. utility accommodation
3. roadside highway facilities

The Roadside Vegetation Management Policy establishes future practices to manage the vegetation along Wisconsin's roadsides. Other policies or plans address, or will address the other policy areas of highway roadsides.

There are seven major component parts that are central to a comprehensive and effective policy on roadside vegetation management. They are, the highway system, vegetation, beauty and aesthetics, wildlife, vegetation management, types of vegetation inventory, and vegetation management plans.

BACKGROUND

Formal roadside vegetation management by WiDOT began in 1931. At that time, the seed specifications for roadside planting called for agriculturally oriented seed mixes and maintenance by mowing, burning or harvesting. Roadside vegetation policy evolved through the years to include seed mixes of lawn type grasses, mowing and/or herbicide use for better control of the landscape.

WiDOT's vegetation policy has been heavily influenced by economics. In 1962, AASHTO revised maintenance guidelines to reduce mowing as herbicide became easier and less expensive to use. The 1973 and 1978 oil crises and decreased fuel tax revenues negatively impacted highway maintenance budgets. WiDOT drastically reduced mowing to the ditch line and 30 feet out from the edge of pavement once every three years.

Though fuel oil costs and supply still influence roadside vegetation management, environmental preservation has become an overriding concern. In 1983, WiDOT drastically reduced herbicide use in compliance with State ground water protection legislation and Federal hazardous material legislation. Concurrently, there was growing concern that early disturbances to roadsides (mowing before August 1) destroys thousands of wildlife nests and nesting sites annually. Thus, the time had come for a comprehensive review of the roadside management policy.

THE HIGHWAY SYSTEM

The term "highway system" frequently refers to state highways, which are signed and numbered as Interstate, Federal and State highways. However, the highway user is not limited to cross country travel on state highways. The motorist has access to other roads and freely changes from cross country travel on state highways to distribution and land access travel on county and town roads. Within the densely populated urban areas, the urban traveler has similar freedom to travel on the arterial, collector and local streets that urban "systems" provide.

State highways are principally rural facilities that are conceived, designed, constructed and maintained to move people, goods and services from place to places safely and efficiently. User comfort and enjoyment is also a goal and result of highway development and operation.

Early roads in the United States were merely paths or trails from point to point along the route of least resistance. When roads were improved by grading to accommodate wheeled vehicles, it became evident that in order to maintain a constant width of surface, additional land along the roadside was needed to accommodate cuts and fills. Gradually, the advantage of having control over this land became evident and the practice of owning or leasing land beyond the edge of the roadway became policy.

Eventually, paved surfaces replaced gravel roads, shoulders were added for additional safety and roadsides became part of every highway. Presently, highway right-of-way widths range from 48 feet to 350 feet or more. Today's highways perform the same functions as earlier roads; but, they are designed, constructed and maintained to carry large volumes of light and heavy vehicles at high speeds.

As motoring for pleasure became popular and the concept of scenic highways evolved, the aesthetics of highway design took on greater significance. Roadsides became the medium for fitting the highway to the terrain. Roadsides acted as the transition zone between the linear geometric regularity of the highway and their adjacent lands.

VEGETATION

In the early 1800s, prior to European settlement, Wisconsin's landscape was covered with a wide variety of vegetation communities, including, northern and southern hardwood forest, oak savannas, pine barrens, and prairie grasslands. For example, northern hardwood forests of red maple, hemlock, yellow birch, etc. covered 48% of the total land surface in the state oak savannas covered over 21% and prairie grasses covered 6%. However, native vegetation of pre-European settlement times is quickly disappearing. Today less than 2,000 acres of the original 2.1 million acres of native Prairie remain.

Human development of the land was

devastating to native plant communities, especially during the post war period of improved technologies. Agriculture and suburbanization caused the greatest damage by penetrating deep into the natural landscape. Highway construction for the interstate system accelerated in the 1960s and required expansive rights-of-way. The end result of all these forces was the destruction of thousands of acres of forest, wetland and prairie.

In response to the need for quick and economical stabilization of large areas disturbed by construction activities, a variety of "exotic" or nonnative trees, shrubs and grasses became the traditional solution for soil stabilization and vegetative cover along roadsides. Nonnative species such as Colorado Blue Spruce, Crown vetch, and Kentucky Bluegrass were introduced, transforming the native landscape into a tidy, visually uninteresting and ecologically unstable roadside.

Nonnative plants were promoted as the new and better solution. They were commercially available and familiar. While native seed and plant sources for Big Bluestem, Black-eyed Susan, dogwood, and oaks were in short supply or difficult to transplant, nonnatives were now familiar members of the local nurseries and residential landscapes.

The use of nonnative plants over time offers a sobering and valuable lesson. Excessive labor, energy and environmental costs are required to sustain a vegetation policy based largely on nonnative plant species. An improved roadside vegetation policy is overdue and must strike a more equitable balance between functional, aesthetic, and environmental considerations.

The concept of "natural roadsides" is not new. "Natural roadsides" refer to roadsides that contain undisturbed or re-established native plant communities and land forms existing before 1840.

As early as 1975, Wisconsin began implementing pilot projects which reintroduced native vegetation back into roadsides. Fifteen counties have already benefited from these projects. Other Midwestern states such as Minnesota, Iowa and Illinois have joined Wisconsin in the search for answers to similar roadside vegetation problems. Interestingly, each has returned to a native plant solution, looking to the past and discovering answers for the future.

Native vegetation offers many benefits to highway managers, motorists and wildlife. Perhaps the single greatest advantage is protection of the highway facility through long term prevention of soil erosion. Limited mowing, encourages thick deep roots to anchor the soil along roadsides. Furthermore, native plants tolerate the wide range of soil types and climatic conditions present in Wisconsin. The variety and adaptability of native vegetation can sustain cover through adverse growing conditions.

The variety present in natural roadsides also offers motorists a rich aesthetic landscape, full of textures and colors enhanced by seasonal changes. Finally, native plants provide much needed habitat for wildlife. Roadsides have become nesting grounds for birds and small animals because they are relatively undisturbed areas.

Highway managers have relied on mowing to control woody plants for safety purposes. However, research shows that short mowing actually stresses the plant and weakens the root system, thereby increasing soil erosion. Additionally, lawn or turf grasses used for roadside cover do not perform well over thousands of highway miles with varying soil types and growing conditions found in Wisconsin. The use of nonnative grasses, in conjunction with mowing, has created unstable roadsides with potentially dangerous consequences for the highway facility. Thus, WiDOT policy now limits regular mowing to a 10 foot pass from the shoulder, of not less than 6 inches high.

The central goal of the roadside vegetation policy for the 1990s is preservation and reestablishment of "native vegetation" in support of functional highway needs. The benefits of pursuing this policy far exceed the labor, energy, and environmental costs required to sustain a vegetation policy based largely on nonnative plant species.

BEAUTY AND AESTHETICS

Beauty and aesthetics are two of many factors involved in roadside design. Second only to safety, they are two of the most important from the motorist's point of view. Roads provide a viewpoint from which the country is most often seen as they form a network over the face of the land. It has been estimated that at least one-third of all motor travel is for social, recreational or vacation purposes, and driving for pleasure is nation's most important outdoor recreational activity.

As early as 1949, legislation advanced a nationwide interest to preserve and protect the natural beauty of the Mississippi River Valley for the motoring public. Scenic, recreational and local traffic factors unique to this corridor were recognized when preliminary planning began for a parkway. Modifications to the geometric standards were accepted by the United States Congress, and charged to the Mississippi River Parkway Planning Commission for implementation.

During the 1960s, federal legislation addressed highway aesthetics. The United States Department of Transportation Act of 1966 declared it national policy to preserve, where possible, the "natural beauty of the countryside, public parks and recreation lands, wildlife and waterfowl refuges, and historic sites."

More than any other country, ours is an automobile society. For most Americans, the automobile is a principal instrument of transportation, work, daily activity, vacation and pleasure. By making our roads and highways to the enjoyment of nature and beauty, we can greatly enrich the life of nearly all our people in city and countryside alike... Our task is twofold. First, to ensure that roads themselves are not destructive of nature and natural beauty. Second, to make our roads ways to recreation and pleasure.

President Lyndon Johnson
1966 Message on Natural Beauty to the Congress of the United States

In 1969, the National Environmental Policy Act expanded national policy to "encourage productive and enjoyable harmony between man and his environment." Furthermore, the Act requires Environmental Impact Statements for all federal projects significantly affecting the environment -- including highways. These provisions include all locales, not just rural areas or woodlands.

In 1987, national legislation was enacted directing the use of native wildflowers along federally aided highway projects under Section 136 of the Surface Transportation and Uniform Relocation Act.

In conjunction with legislation, public opinion has changed over time as highway systems develop and expand. Americans are more environmentally conscious and thus expect more from the highway system. No longer are motorists content with ribbons of concrete cutting through the landscape to get from point A to point B. Roadway travelers expect diverse, panoramic views and broad curving highways, in addition to interesting and graceful routes.

WILDLIFE

Modern land use practices have done much to destroy wildlife habitat. The change from "horse" power to "horse power" enabled a single farmer to increase the land on which he produces crops from several acres to several hundred acres. As farm machinery evolved unto larger, more powerful equipment, the farmer found it expeditious to enlarge his fields by removing fence rows and farm lanes between fields, making one large field out of several smaller ones.

By doing so, the farmer destroyed some of the prime habitat and nesting cover used by wildlife. Other changes in farming practices such as using herbicides in row crops to eliminate weeds and earlier mowing of hay have also taken their toll. Government programs aimed at controlling crop production, such as the current "set-aside" program, are often hailed as a boon to wildlife but are temporary in nature and subject to change with every change in program.

This change has not been limited to "horse" power. The farmer's exodus to the city has enabled developers to convert agricultural fields to housing tracts and shopping centers. This conversion has reduced wildlife habitat even further. Regarding changing land use patterns, a report entitled "Managing Minnesota's Farmland Roadsides: A Case Study In Wildlife Management" says:

> Marshes have been drained, burned and filled. Wood lots have been cleared. Diverse agriculture has been replaced by extensive planting of row crops . . . which offer poor shelter for wildlife. Fall plowing has sharply reduced the amount and quality of food and shelter in cultivated areas. Chemical fertilizers have reduced the need for crop rotation, a system which left hay fields available to wildlife.

As land available for wildlife habitat continues to shrink, the importance of roadside management policies increase. This importance is directly related to the relative permanence of wide and even distribution of highway rights-of-way.

Historically, the standard practice for managing roadside grasses has been mowing. Over the years, the number of acres mowed and the number of mowing cycles per season have been curtailed. While the reduction in acres mowed provided more land suitable for habitat, the timing of the mowing cycles still precluded development of ideal habitat condition.

In 1989, WiDOT moved to correct this situation by adopting a policy which allowed most mowing more than ten feet from the edge of the shoulder only during the month of August. The new schedule enables those species of birds which nest in grasslands to complete their nesting cycle before the grass cover is mowed. The grasses regrow later in the fall and provide residual nesting cover required for the next spring.

The roadside, with its variety of trees, shrubs and grasses, has tremendous potential to be used by wildlife. Currently, this potential is not fully realized. All animals and birds are negatively affected by lack of habitat. This could be remedied with positive decisions involving management of their habitat.

WiDOT has planted shrub hedgerows, native grasses and forbs for beautification, restoration, snowdrift control, etc. Presently, the creation of wildlife habitat is an equally valid reason.

Wildlife populations can be directly affected by maintenance practices on roadsides. The report from Minnesota notes that "wildlife researchers once believed that roadsides were only used for nesting when other cover was not available. Now they know that many nesting animals favor roadsides over other cover types . . ." As off-right-of-way habitat continues to dwindle and highway right-of-way remains fairly permanent, roadsides may become corridors for migration.

VEGETATION MANAGEMENT

Prior to 1931, abutting highway property owners were responsible for maintaining roadside vegetation. Most roadsides were in agriculture or commercial use. If not in use, the roadsides probably were covered with native vegetation.

Formal management by WiDOT of state highway roadside in Wisconsin began in 1931. In those early roadside management days, mowing was the principal tool. Burning, using WPA crews was also used to control vegetation. The 1931 WiDOT seed specification called for agriculture oriented mixes of Rye, Oats, Timothy and Alsike Clover.

In 1935, the seed specification was revised and set up for four soul types. The mixes included Redtop, Kentucky Bluegrass, Timothy, Red Clover, Alsike Clover and Alfalfa. These mixes moved the seed more toward turf type and/or lawn grasses.

Cutting, scything and mowing became standard practice and all mowable roadsides were cut. Mowing probably served as a form of weed control to aid neighboring farmers. Or perhaps, the European influence with their controlled landscape became the objective measure of beauty. The 1941 seed specification continued the trend toward lawn type cover with the addition of Colonial Bentgrass and Ryegrass to the mixes.

In 1951, the seed specification was simplified by dropping the alfalfa, sand vetch, and colonial bent. The removal of alfalfa and sand vetch are evidence of emphasis on lawn type mixes. The colonial bent does not mix well with other grasses and was probably problem on roadsides.

In 1957, the seed specifications were revised and Red Fescue replaced Timothy in the mixes. The mixes were also reduced to two. In 1963, Kentucky 31 Fescue was introduced as more tolerant of adverse conditions and good for steep slopes.

During the 1957-1963 time period much nationwide highway roadside management discussion centered on reduction in mowing and preservation of native vegetation. Also, during this time period herbicides were easier and cheaper that mowing as a means of controlling roadside vegetation. In 1962, AASHTO revised the maintenance mowing guide and called for reduced mowing.

Highway roadside vegetation management policy from 1930 to 1960 resulted in the peak effort to control the landscape using western European ideals. Most of the roadside was mowed, except very steep slopes. Selective and broadcast methods of spraying pesticides were employed. Selective spraying killed the vegetation around guard rail posts. The entire roadside was sprayed to kill broadleaf weeds. Growth retardants were used to slow vegetation growth in areas difficult to mow. In 1969, the Wisconsin roadside seed mixes included nine species in five different mixes, including Birdsfoot Trefoil and crown vetch.

The 1973 and 1978 oil embargoes resulted in significantly higher gas costs as less fuel was available. Less fuel caused a funding short fall in the Transportation Fund. Accordingly, there were significant reductions in the state highway budget, including highway maintenance. The budgets for mowing and herbicide vegetation control were significantly reduced also.

The resultant roadside mowing policy permitted mowing out to the ditch line. From the ditch line to the edge of the right-of-way was not to be mowed or sprayed, except for noxious weeds. The policy encouraged growth of existing vegetation, as well as natural development of existing native vegetation in this area. This was a drastic change, especially at interchange areas which were completely mowed. The herbicide budget was reduced but the policy did not change.

In 1981, Red Top and Alsike Clover were dropped from the WiDOT seed specifications. Also during the early 1980s, "safety clear zones" were emphasized to improve safety for errant vehicles. The clear zone is to be kept free of woody vegetation and fixed objects that increase damage and injury on impact.

In 1983, Wisconsin enacted major ground water protection legislation. At the same time federal hazardous material legislation was being implemented. Wisconsin legislation requires commercial applicators of herbicides to be licensed and certified; state laws exempt county highway maintenance personnel from licensing, but requires certification. The laws also restrict pesticide use. The impact of these laws demanded a comprehensive review of roadside vegetation management practices. Reduced spraying will require less planting of turf grasses and a desirable return to deep rooted native vegetation.

As stated earlier, there was considerable concern that early disturbances to roadsides destroy thousands of nests and nesting sites annually. The most serious factor adversely affecting wildlife production is mowing before August 1.

In 1989, after considerable review and discussion, WiDOT modified its roadside mowing policy:

- Mow +/- 10 foot shoulder cuts as needed. Mow vision corners as needed for traffic safety.
- Mow other areas according to current policy, but only during the month of August.

    1 mowing pass over fill slopes

    1 mowing pass beyond the ditch line

    Mow out to the clear zone once every three years

- Limited herbicide spot spraying may continue until existing inventory of purchased material is exhausted. Additional herbicide purchases must be justified.

This new policy was also established as a pilot project for native vegetation research and mowing equipment performance analysis. Based on actual field experiences in 1989 and another period of discussion, an updated mowing policy will be formulated for 1990.

INVENTORIES

> There are many wildflowers native to Wisconsin which are a source of pleasure to all travelers and should, therefore, be preserved. ... We must be alert to preserve all that can be preserved. ... The problem of proper attention to roadside planting, involving the preservation of good plants and the destruction of noxious weeds, is one phase of the large problems of (highway) maintenance.
>
> 1916 Biennial Report of the
> Wisconsin Highway Commission

These phrases, published 75 years ago, seem to voice many of today's concerns. Thus, the goal remains to preserve what is acknowledged as a valuable resource and to preserve that which is pleasurable for the viewer.

Facts about existing roadside vegetation along Wisconsin's state highways should be known and recorded before statewide and site specific plans can be developed and implemented. Current data related to roadside plants exists only as a prerequisite to, or as the result of, a highway improvement project. These are site-specific project inventories and cover only a few miles of the ,400 center-line miles of state highways. There are other existing vegetation database resources that can provide facts or factual premises for this planning effort:

- Robert W. Finley's map, the "Original Vegetation Cover of Wisconsin," a 1976 compilation of notes from the U.S. General Land Office.
- John T. Curtis's map, "Major Plant Communities of Wisconsin," ca. 1840. 1970s WDNR Natural Heritage Data Base
- County Inventories of Native Vegetation.
- University of Wisconsin, College of Agriculture, School of Landscape Architecture's records on railroad and roadsides in southern Wisconsin.
- Various private citizens who have inventoried native vegetation along roadsides, including: "Citizens and Me," reports from Cy Kabut Vera Stroud Inventory of Waukesha County, and others.

This fact-gathering process is called an "inventory."

VEGETATION MANAGEMENT PLANS

An inventory of the 150,000 acres of Wisconsin's state trunk highway roadsides is needed to provide a factual base for planning vegetation improvements and maintenance. Vegetation management plans for segments of highways will be the product of this comprehensive process. These segment plans will be synthesized and prioritized into a six-year vegetation enhancement program that will:

1. Save valuable native plant remnants,
2. Initiate modern roadside vegetation maintenance to improve the quality and quantity of native vegetation, and
3. Improve the visual quality of the roadside through appropriate landscape planting.

This plan will be tailored for all highways within their respective ecological regions.

Highway Inventory Segments

The roadside inventory shall be conducted on aerial photograph strip maps created from available widow coverage photography. The aerial photograph strip maps shall be the base map during the inventory.

Roadside Vegetation Data Elements

The roadside inventory should identify and classify the data elements defined in the inventory:

1. general plant species
2. critical plant species
3. native plant community
4. suggested enhancements
5. terrain
6. adjacent land uses
7. significant land forms
8. general soil type

SUMMARY

Roadsides can have their own inherent beauty, but should also complement or enhance what lies beyond the edge of the right-of-way, and not compete with Wisconsin's visual variety. Since the roadside is in the motorist's field-of-view, it should accentuate the whole viewscape. To meet the state roadside vegetation demands into the 21st century state highway managers must develop detailed vegetation management plans. These plans must be based on detailed vegetation inventories and appropriate vegetation management techniques. Finally, the vegetation management plan must reflect and enhance the aesthetics, the wildlife, and the vegetation of the surrounding area, while providing safe driving conditions along the highway system.

Selection of Alternative Routes for the Southern Extension of the New River Parkway

Sarah Duncan and William E. Shepherd

The New River Parkway is a planned, 2-lane, scenic byway through 50 miles of the middle New River basin. The middle New River basin is described as the watershed area into the New River from the boundary between Virginia and West Virginia, up to the New River Gorge in West Virginia.

This area is filled with state and national parks which testify to the scenic significance of the area and its natural, recreational, and cultural resources. The New River Parkway was conceived to link these resources in a way that provides a pleasant, leisurely driving experience.

In 1987, the proposed route of the parkway, which extended from Interstate 64 through the New River Gorge National River to Hinton, West Virginia, was extended south in order to better serve other recreational facilities important to the area. This southern extension begins at the mouth of the Bluestone River and ends with a connection to Interstate 77, the West Virginia Turnpike in the vicinity of Princeton. This extension will also make the parkway an important link between two major interstate highways (Interstate 64 and Interstate 77).

Unlike the northern and central segments of the parkway, which are confined to the narrow bottom lands along the rivers, the southern extension must traverse a huge and varied land area bounded by the Bluestone River Gorge to the north, Federal Route 460 to the south, the New River Gorge to the east, and Interstate 77 to the west. Because this area is so large and contains so many different landscapes ranging from high plateaus to deep gorges, a variety of possible parkway routes could be developed.

A procedure, therefore, had to be developed for the inventory, analysis, and evaluation of this landscape so that areas with the greatest potential could be realized, which would aid in the selection of general parkway routes. It should be emphasized at this point, that the goal was to select general routes and not a specific alignment. The procedure developed by Virginia Tech involved community participation, a scenic assessment of the area, and a resource inventory done in conjunction with Southern West Virginia Research Associates.

The procedure began with community meetings. People of the local community were invited to suggest possible parkway routes and to point out areas of significance. Many of these people had lived in the area all their lives and were from families who had occupied land in the area for generations. Consequently, these residents were very familiar with the terrain, history, features, and network of existing roads in the area. Their suggestions and comments gave insight and provided the researchers with a more in-depth understanding of the area.

The next step involved conducting a scenic assessment. The purpose of the scenic assessment was to identify the scenic value of different areas within the study area. The most scenic areas would be better suited for the parkway since the parkway's intent is to provide visitors with a scenic driving experience. This assessment began with a study of the physiographic characteristics of the area, that is, characteristics related to the land form, elevation, and drainage patterns. These characteristics were studied in the field and with hypsographic maps, which are maps with different colors representing different elevations. The coloring makes it easier to see the shapes and changes of the land. From these studies, the area was divided into different physiographic units. Fourteen different physiographic units were identified in the area. They ranged from knobs and plateaus to creek bottoms and river gorges.

SCENIC VALUES

Next, the scenic value of each physiographic unit was determined. Scenic evaluations were made using a scoring system. Landscapes were rated as they appeared during the spring and fall months when tourist activity is greatest in the area. Each unit was rated on a scale from 0 to 5 for the following elements.

View

Existing or potential background views were favored in the scoring. These are the distant, blue views that are often found at overlooks or pull-offs. They are generally considered very scenic. The more background views in a unit and the greater the potential for background views in a unit, the higher the score in this category.

Water Resources

Water can add visual interest to a scene and, in the case of large water bodies, it can help to unify a scene. A number of studies, in fact, indicate a human preference for landscapes with water. Conspicuous water bodies, such as a lake or a river, therefore, received the highest scores. Creeks and streams, which were more common to many of the units, received mid-ranged scores.

Landforms

Unusual or spectacular landforms, such as the river gorges, which range in depth from 800' to over 1000', received high scores. Also receiving high scores were landforms which provide for more variety in the experience of them, such as the hill and valley areas where the experience is always changing as one winds over and around the landforms.

Color

Color is difficult to evaluate because it is always changing. Most of this change, however, is in the plant material itself and not so much in the rocks, soils, bark, etc. Color was therefore scored according to the color-giving elements in the unit. Color giving elements include:

1. Distant Views—They add the colors blue or purple to the palette.

2. Land Uses—Fields, for example, can add yellow, while forests are a darker green.

3. Rock Formations—Prominent rock features such as the cliff faces found in the river gorges, often add different colors the palette of the unit.

4. Plant Materials—Generally, the colors of plant materials are fairly predictable. In the summer forests are green; in the fall, they are a mix of brown, red, yellow and orange; in the winter they are grey and brown. Spring is the most difficult to predict. Understory trees and shrubs can add conspicuous accents of white, purple, and pink. Some units may contain more of these conspicuous flowering plants than others. The more these plants can be identified, the more complete the score under this category will be.

Scenic Integrity

This general score was based on the researchers impressions of the unit as they viewed it and experienced it. Consideration was given to how consistent the quality of the scenery was and what potentials existed.

An overall scenic score for each unit was calculated by adding the scores of each of the above five categories. The higher the overall score, the more scenic the landscape of that unit was considered.

PARKWAY POTENTIAL SCORES

After realizing the scenic values of the study area, other factors important to the concept of the parkway had to be considered. Each unit was, therefore, reevaluated according to the factors that would make it more suitable for a parkway. The "parkway potential" of each unit was determined by rating from 0 to 3 the quality and quantity of the following elements.

Recreation Resources

The more existing national, state, or county parks in the unit, the better the score. Also receiving high scores were units with high occurrences of resources such as streams which could potentially support recreational activities.

Historic Features

Many historical features exist in the study area. These have the potential to become a point of interest along the parkway. Historic features could include:

1. Historic Structures—Structures in good condition are favored.
2. Cemeteries—Those associated with churches or private family plots, which are very common in the area, are of historical importance.
3. Historic Locations—These are places where, possibly, a significant event took place. This could include turnpike routes, ferry crossings, and settlement areas. Archaeological sites were not considered a potential resource for the parkway because they are to be kept hidden for their own protection. Consequently, they were not scored in this evaluation.

Land Use

Land uses compatible with the parkway are those which support the tourist-related economic, recreational, scenic, and historic goals and objectives of the parkway concept plan. Most of the area is forest, farms, and scattered residences, all of which are compatible with the parkway. Land uses considered incompatible with the parkway were commercial uses located along heavily traveled roadways. These commercial uses were mostly oriented toward the needs of the local resident. They included auto dealerships, schools, and video shops.

Scenery

The results of the scenic assessment were used here. If a unit's scenic score fell into the top 1/3 bracket, it received a high parkway potential score.

Natural Features

These are features which might add interest. Natural features include, but are not limited to, waterfalls, prominent cliff faces, and unusual plant communities. Rare, threatened, and endangered plant sites were not evaluated as an attraction. Rather, they were to be avoided for their own protection; so they were not scored.

The overall parkway potential for each unit was realized by adding the scores from each category. In order to confirm the results of this procedure, interested citizens were also invited to score the units. Everyone generally agreed that the Bluestone and New River Gorges, and the ridges and rugged lowlands near them had the most potential to support the purposes of the parkway.

Three alternative corridors for the southern extension of the New River Parkway were selected based on the results of this procedure. Subsequent review of these alternatives by the New River parkway Authority, civic groups, and interested citizens resulted in the recommendation of two alternatives.

Alternative 1 is oriented toward the New River Gorge in the eastern portion of the study area. It provides for variety in the experience as it follows ridges overlooking the gorge, valley farms, the bottom lands along the river, and high plateaus. This alternative terminates at the newly constructed West Virginia Tourist Information Center near the intersection of Interstate 77 and Federal Route 460.

Alternative 2 is oriented toward the Bluestone River Gorge in the western portion of the study area. It is a more direct route which mainly follows the Tallery Mountain plateau and its edge, where the views into the Bluestone River Gorge are outstanding. As it descends off the plateau into the rugged lowlands, it makes a direct connection with Interstate 77.

Both alternatives are described in further depth in the New River Parkway Concept Plan. This plan also describes in greater detail, the purpose and intent of the New River Parkway along with the goals and objectives of the New River Parkway Authority.

Concept Plan for the New River Parkway

William E. Shepherd and Sarah Duncan

Project Description

The New River Parkway is a planned 50 mile scenic byway utilizing existing and new roadways in the middle New River basin of southern West Virginia. The Parkway will serve as the southern gateway to the New River Gorge National River and unite major recreational and cultural facilities along the New and Bluestone Rivers into a scenic road system. The Parkway is being designed as a two lane touring parkway through a defined "parkway corridor" which will include compatible private uses, commercial services and public recreational facilities near or adjacent to the roadway.

The parkway is envisioned as a scenic roadway linking rich and diverse historical, cultural, scenic and natural resources together with local communities throughout the region. While the New River Parkway will link major recreational facilities, it holds the potential to serve as a principle recreational amenity for the motoring public. The intent of the parkway is to provide a pleasant leisurely driving experience along the New River, Bluestone Lake and through the rolling uplands of the surrounding Allegheny plateau.

A master plan for the New River Parkway is currently being developed by the New River Parkway Authority. In accord with this plan, the parkway will be designed to improve river access, enhance the quality of scenery, provide recreational opportunities, protect compatible rural uses, conserve and protect sensitive habitats, and encourage new tourism-oriented facilities and business. All lands within 500 feet of the parkway will be subject to the policies and regulations of the parkway master plan and land management system of the New River Parkway Authority.

Parkway facilities will include safety pullouts, scenic overlooks, rest areas, accessways, trails, bikeways, historic/cultural sites, recreational areas, habitat preserves and scenic management areas.

Project Setting

The project is located in Raleigh, Summers, and Mercer Counties of southern West Virginia within the immediate watershed of the middle New River basin. Adjacent larger communities include Beckley, Princeton and Bluefield, West Virginia. Smaller communities with more direct access to the Parkway include Hinton, Pipestem, Lerona and Athens. While historically remote and isolated, this region of West Virginia is within a day's drive (500 miles) of 65% of the entire population of the United States.

The middle New River basin is generally that watershed area from the boundary between Virginia and West Virginia to the south and the great gorge of the New River to the north near Laurel Creek in Fayette County. Principle rivers within this basin which contribute to the New include the Bluestone River from the west and the Greenbrier River to the east.

Physiographically this basin is part of the Allegheny plateau which consists of at least two peneplains which have been deeply dissected by the New River and its major tributaries. Upper surfaces are remnants of rolling plateaus and knobs which have been divided and cut by the ancient drainage system. Narrow river valleys, riverine bottomlands, and hollows closely follow the intricate drainage pattern leaving most of the land in steeply sloping ridges and gorges.

A Partnership for Beauty and Progress

This rugged landscape of the Appalachian Highlands has served as a barrier to movement and communication fostering a sense of isolation for those hardy pioneers who first settled along the New River and its tributaries. This region, first settled in the late 18th century, is a wellspring of Appalachian culture.

Planning Background

In 1978, Congress passed legislation (Public Law 95-625) creating the New River Gorge National River "for the purpose of conserving and interpreting outstanding natural, scenic, and historic values and objects in and around the New River Gorge and preserving as a free-flowing stream an important segment of the New River in West Virginia for the benefit and enjoyment of present and future generations." Recognition of the national importance of the resources of the New River led to increased interest in the cultural assets and recreational opportunities within the middle New River basin.

The concept of a Parkway or touring road along the New River evolved over a period of five years or more. Initially ideas were put forth for the upgrade and improvement of Route 26 which serves the west side area along the New River where most of the park's facilities are located. Heavy visitation of park facilities has caused traffic problems on this narrow country road.

In 1985, with the strong support of local representation, the West Virginia Legislature passed legislation formally creating the New River Parkway Authority to oversee the planning of the Parkway. The legislation called for the Parkway Authority to coordinate with governmental agencies, public and private corporations, organizations and individuals "for planning, assisting and establishing recreational tourism, industrial, economic and community development of the New River Parkway for the benefit of West Virginians."

Additional powers and responsibilities were given to the Parkway Authority by the West Virginia Legislature in 1988 "to develop and set for land-use regulations minimum performance standards which are necessary to implement the Authority's plan or plans" within a scenic corridor extending 500 feet of either side of the roadway.

Present membership of the Authority includes three voting members from Raleigh, Summers, and Mercer Counties appointed by their respective County Commissions. Nonvoting members include representatives from the New River Gorge National River, U.S. Army Corps of Engineers and West Virginia Divisions of Transportation, Commerce, Agriculture, and Natural Resources.

The New River Parkway Authority prepared the original concept plan (1987) for the Parkway which focused on a 24 mile long scenic route running from newly completed Interstate 64 south along Route 26, the Hinton Bypass (Route 3), and Route 20 to Pipestem State Park near the Mercer County line. This plan described how existing areas could be enhanced and new facilities developed for visitors and local residents along with the actions needed to implement the plan.

On the basis of the goals of the original concept plan, the Surface Transportation and Uniform Relocation Assistance Act of 1987 (Public Law 100-17) authorized the expenditure of $17.6 million to construct a portion of the New River Parkway in accordance with the recommendations of the New River Parkway Authority for the purpose of demonstrating benefits to recreation, tourism, and industrial, economic, and community development.

As the Parkway Authority initiated preliminary engineering studies of possible alignments and future traffic patterns, it became apparent that the Parkway could not provide adequate access and circulation to all of the recreational facilities it was intended to serve. As a result of these studies the proposed route of the parkway was extended by the Parkway Authority to link with Interstate 77, the West Virginia Turnpike, in the vicinity of Princeton.

This extension facilitates connection to the two major interstate highways within the region providing the necessary access and circulation to existing and proposed recreational and cultural facilities within the basin.

The Bluestone National Scenic River, which includes a major segment of the lower Bluestone River and Gorge between Pipestem and Bluestone State Parks, came under New River Gorge management in 1988. Interpretive activities were begun in 1989 with general management and land protection planning currently being developed as this newest of national recreation facilities begins operation.

The Parkway will provide direct access to this Scenic River, linking it with the New River Gorge National River.

In 1989 the Parkway Authority contracted with Virginia Polytechnic Institute and State University (Virginia Tech) to prepare a Master Plan and Land Management System for the New River Parkway. Through community participation and the cooperative efforts of many agencies and local governments, the Parkway Authority developed goals and objectives to locate and construct the Parkway and properly control land use within its scenic corridor. Policies derived from these goals and objectives will be implemented through a comprehensive land management system to encourage compatible land use while protecting the scenic corridor.

In 1990 the Parkway Authority requested Virginia Tech and Southern West Virginia Research Associates to prepare a Scenic Corridor Assessment of the entire Parkway from Interstate 64 to Interstate 77 with specific consideration given to the study of alternative routes for the southern extension of the Parkway. This research was preparatory to the development of a comprehensive concept plan for the entire New River Parkway. This overall concept plan has been developed through the cooperative effort of West Virginia Department of Transportation, Southern West Virginia Research Associates, and Virginia Tech.

The West Virginia Department of Transportation recently has completed the necessary engineering studies for a number of alternative parkway alignments for the first phase of construction from Interstate 64 to the Hinton Bypass. This portion of the Parkway has required the most complex and careful design as it must balance the diverse considerations for wildlife habitat, riverine wetlands, scenic qualities, and rural settlements along the margins to the river. A draft environmental impact statement has been being prepared for this section from Interstate 64 to Hinton which assesses the preferred Parkway alignment along with other possible alternatives.

Cultural and Natural Resources

The cultural and natural resources of the middle New River basin are many and varied. In large measure, they are unspoiled by changing land use patterns and the pressures of rapid urbanization. With the exception of the industrial boom in the late 18th and early 19th centuries, the region remains little changed. Recent urbanization followed the wave of secondary highways built in the late 1940s and early 1950s. For the most part these highways bypassed much of this region, following more easily traversed terrain. The settlements and farms in remote ridges, valleys, and narrow bottoms remain much as they were many years ago. The history of this region is evident in the cultural and natural landscape of today.

The Cultural Landscape

The New River has, over the centuries, carved a magnificent gorge into the steep mountains of West Virginia. The river also left its impression on the people living near it. Not only did they learn to work with the river, but they also became like the river, hardy and determined to exist in this isolated region.

The earliest Indian settlers dating back to 10,500 B.C., found the land to be rich with deer, wild turkey and buffalo. It was a common hunting ground for many of the tribes that lived near the area. The numerous salt springs attracted the wildlife and were highly valued by the Indians. It was often in the quest of salt springs that native tribes came into deadly combat with each other and later with pioneer settlers who migrated from Virginia.

No permanent Indian settlements existed in this region of the Appalachian Highlands at the time the white pioneers began to move in. The Shawnee, Cherokee, Creek, and Chocktaw tribes that roamed the lands along the New River lived to the north and south of this region. Major Indian trails followed the New River and served as a link between the Warrior's trail (later the Wilderness Road) in the ridge and valley province to the southeast and the Ohio River basin to the northwest. A network of trails also connected the Greenbrier valley with the Bluestone Gorge and the southern Appalachian Highlands to the southwest. There is evidence, however, that great numbers of Indians had, at an earlier time, inhabited villages along the New and Greenbrier Rivers. Crumps Bottom contains significant archaeological sites where some of these villages existed around 1200-1671 A.D.

The first white settlements were established by the families of George Washington's militia coming from regions in Virginia. They first settled in the Greenbrier Valley along the eastern drainage of the middle New River basin establishing a number of small forts and fortified settlements.

These settlers were tough and self-reliant, withstanding the forces of nature, isolation, American wars, and frequent raids by Indians, particularly the Shawnee.

Many of the Indian trails developed into the first roads and later into important turnpikes. The rugged terrain of the middle New River basin made travel and the construction of roads extremely difficult. The Red Sulphur Springs Turnpike, one of the first roads through the basin, became an important route to the salt industry. In 1850 the Mercer Salt Works were established at the springs near Lick Creek. The salt was carried along the turnpike to the New River where it was transported across Shanklin's Ferry. The bustling community that developed near the ferry boasted a general store, post office, blacksmith shop, and water mill.

The Civil War proved to be especially difficult for the families living in the New River basin. Much of what was grown in the area was used to feed the Confederate troops, and people were torn between the north and the south. Some of the places along the New River were renamed during the Civil War. Bull Falls, near Crumps Bottom, was renamed Warford when the locals directed the Federals to this rough part of the river for crossing.

Historically, people living in this area survived by hunting and farming in the narrow bench of lowlands near the river. Until the 1800s, the river was the only reliable form of transportation. People living in the area depended on the river for their livelihood and connection to the outside world and consequently developed a strong, lasting bond with it. This bond is still felt by residents today.

Because of their isolation, people living in the area have always had to make the most of what they had. Most of what was bought, coffee, tea, and salt was bartered, that is, paid in exchange for their own farm products. One mill usually served several small communities. The oldest mills were water powered, being built on the New River itself, or on one of its many tributaries. Cooper's Mill still stands along a remote section of the Bluestone River deep within the gorge. The remains of other mills can still be found, such as the mill at Pipestem and the one along Pipestem Creek to the north. After 1952, the local mills began to close in favor of the larger, more advanced milling companies found in Hinton and Princeton.

Ferries were also common on the New River as they served as the only crossings for wagons and their passengers. The ferries no longer exist on the New River, which some believe is a tragedy. Their extinction greatly impacted the social fabric and cultural flavor of the area.

Travel down river was also common many years ago. The bateaux, a flat, narrow boat maneuvered by long poles reaching to the bottom of the river, was used to carry products from the farms near Crumps Bottom and Indian Creek to the markets in Hinton.

Hinton was not a town with "city slickers" until after 1874 when the Chesapeake and Ohio railroad was completed through the New River Gorge. The railroad was originally built to provide a connection between the Chesapeake Bay and the Ohio country. In making this connection, the railroad followed the New River Gorge from Hinton to the coal producing areas of the gorge in the north. The transportation provided by the railroad helped the coal industry boom and became one of national and international importance.

The success of the coal, railroad, and timber industries was rapid and resulted in many changes, but was unfortunately short-lived. By 1950, much of what had been established was gone or abandoned. Changes in the methods of coal mining, the working out of older mines, the conversion of locomotive power from steam to diesel, and the consumption of the timber resource affected everyone.

Today, the town of Hinton is a trip back in time. Not much has changed in its physical appearance since the 1950s, but in many ways that makes the town special. The cobble streets and the handcrafted buildings are full of the vitality and pride of its heyday. Many of the small, isolated, farming communities that developed around the mills, churches, and general stores remain in the area. Their structures are often in good condition due to their continued use.

The Natural Landscape

The New River, which has been such a force in shaping the people, has also spent eons shaping the land. From its headwaters at Blowing Rock in North Carolina, the New flows north through Virginia and West Virginia. Only in West Virginia, however, has it carved a magnificent gorge into the mountains, ranging in depth from 600 to 1,400 feet, and in width from a half mile to over one mile. The New is considered especially unique, however, because the river flows north and west, perpendicular to the axis of the Appalachian ridge and valley mountain system. For this reason, the New River is considered by most geologists to have existed before the uplift of the Appalachian range, one of the oldest in the world. The cutting of the river through the mountain range as it slowly rose formed the gorges and deep river bottoms that we see today along the New and Bluestone Rivers. The steep walls of the river gorges reveal the geological formations that make up the Appalachian plateau. Because of the northwest tilt of these sedimentary formations, the southern portion of the gorge reveals the older layers, while the deeper, northern portion reveals the younger layers.

While the exact age of the river is unknown, many believe it to be at least 65 million years old. It was once part of a longer river system called the Teays that flowed north through central Ohio, Indiana, and Illinois to the Mississippi River. During the ice age, however, a glacier diverted the waters and created the Ohio and Kanawha Rivers that the New River currently flows into.

The landscape surrounding the New River is diverse and of great beauty. It is comprised of steep mountains, rolling plateaus, narrow canyons, thin ridges, and low-lying valleys. This topographic diversity harbors a wide variety of plant and animal species, many of which are rare in the region and the nation.

The New River itself is the largest warm water stream fishery in West Virginia. At least fifty-eight species of fish inhabit the waters, some of which are game fish, such as large mouth bass, small mouth bass, catfish, muskellunge, walleye, and crappie. Downstream from Hinton, the New River supports seven species of freshwater mussels and an unusual colony of eastern river cooter turtles. These turtles are isolated from the river cooter turtles of the coastal plains and Piedmont of southeastern states, and may represent Pleistocene relics. The abundance and variety of animals can be attributed to the excellent instream and riparian cover found along the New River. Consequently, the entire river has been identified as existing or potential spawning grounds.

The New River Gorge is clearly a unique and valuable natural resource to the entire nation. In recognition of the national significance of this resource, the Federal government has designated 52 miles of the New River Gorge, from the town of Hinton to Fayette Station, as the New River Gorge National River. This designation not only protects the cultural resources and rare natural features, but also makes them available to people who want to interact with and contemplate their rare beauty.

Two of the New River's major tributaries have also been protected by the federal government. The Gauley River, north of the New River Gorge National River has been designated a National Recreation Area because of the class rapids that provide for some of the most spectacular white water rafting in the East. The Bluestone River, south of the New River Gorge National River, has been designated the Bluestone National Scenic River because of the spectacular and rare beauty of this river and gorge. These national lands, along with seven state parks, all within a 30 mile radius, give testimony to the cultural, recreational and ecological significance of the area.

Issues of Cooperative Venture

Development of the Parkway will require a cooperative effort among federal, state, county and local governments working in conjunction with private businesses, landowners, civic organizations, and citizens. The Parkway Authority will serve, on the one hand, as facilitator and coordinator of this community effort and, on the other, as implementer of land-use policies on private development through the Land Management System.

To achieve a consistent level of mutual cooperation will require that all members of the Authority, voting members and nonvoting member agencies, communicate and coordinate their respective planning and management goals and objectives. This is necessary to achieve consistency in purpose and direction for the Parkway itself and all lands, both public and private, within the parkway corridor. Agencies with land-management directives and responsibilities, such as the National Park Service, Army Corps of Engineers, West Virginia Departments of Natural Resources and Transportation, have a special responsibility to ensure that the Parkway Authority is fully informed and involved in all decisions which impact either the Parkway or lands within the parkway corridor.

The legislative mandate of the New River Parkway Authority is to implement a Master Plan and Land Management System controlling and guiding development within the parkway corridor. To this end, all new development within the parkway corridor will be subject to comprehensive standards, design guidelines, plans, and permit procedures to ensure the compatibility of uses and activities and appropriate development. The Parkway Authority will continue to work with counties and local governments to help plan for future growth and change within the region in a partnership role.

The Parkway Authority is also responsible for the recommendation of design standards and route selection of the Parkway. Policies within the Concept Plan and subsequent Master Plan will help shape and guide their recommendation for the alignment and overall design of the Parkway itself.

Many visitors are not aware of the many and varied recreational, scenic, and cultural attractions the New River region has to offer. Promotion of the region as a "destination resort", where families could spend a week pursuing a wide range of activities, is a key to the success of the Parkway and the development of tourism within the region. The Parkway could serve as the accessway to many of these attractions providing a leisurely touring experience for the visitor.

Concern has also been raised about the lack of a centralized facility which could provide information about the many attractions in the region. The Parkway Authority supports the development of a visitor's facility to serve both the New River Parkway, the New River Gorge National River, and other major recreation facilities in the region. Such a facility located on the Parkway would encourage visitor use of the Parkway as a scenic entrance to the New River Gorge National River, Bluestone National Scenic River, Bluestone Public Hunting and Fishing Area, Pipestem State Park, and Bluestone State Park, as well as help to stimulate local businesses.

Liner and debris along the Parkway is considered a major problem by landowners, civic leaders, and visitors to the area. There is need for a more coordinated regional effort to clean up litter along roadsides and debris along the banks of the New River and its tributaries. The Parkway Authority will support and coordinate non-regulatory voluntary programs and educational programs with interested citizens, agencies and organizations. Such efforts can encourage communication and cooperation at the local level to recognize the importance of the recreational and scenic resources of the region.

Issues of Economic Development

The intent of the Parkway Authority is to encourage tourism related development within the region. The New River Parkway has the potential to draw visitors from throughout the United States as well as tourists from other countries who desire to see, firsthand, the rural character and traditional culture of the Appalachian highlands.

The Parkway Authority supports economic development within the region and in particular, businesses, activities, and enterprises which are compatible with the overall goals and objectives of the Concept Plan. The Parkway Authority supports local businesses which offer regional goods and services, hire local residents, and invest in capital venture programs to benefit all West Virginia citizens.

The Parkway Authority supports tourism and related activities within the parkway corridor which are appropriate and compatible with the outdoor recreational facilities and Parkway improvements to be developed. The Parkway Authority will establish standards and guidelines for tourist facilities regarding scenic and environmental impacts. The overriding concern is to ensure that new tourist development be sensitively located and designed, be in scale and harmony with the traditional rural character of the region, and support the function of communities, and contribute to the quality of life of local residents.

New developments should complement, not contrast or destroy, the quality of life and rural character of the landscape. To this end, the Parkway Authority will encourage alternative growth strategies which do not impair the cultural, natural, recreational and aesthetic objectives of the Master Plan and prohibit developments which do not meet the requirements.

Issues of Accessibility to Recreational Resources

A concern of the Parkway Authority, landowners, and community leaders is to find a way to provide safe and appropriate public access to the river and other natural and scenic resources, while protecting the rights of private property. Increased public demand for access to the river and other scenic areas has resulted in an increase in trespass and damage to private properties. As the number of visitors increase, so will the pressure for access to rivers, streams, and wildland habitat areas.

In part, this has been brought about because of a lack of sufficient public facilities and access points to the river and other natural areas. Water-oriented recreation is the largest attraction for visitors to the parkway. Possible water-based recreation activities are many, from sight seeing and picnicking along the river to the more active boating and white water rafting. Increasingly more demand will be felt for a greater range in recreational opportunity and experience along the parkway corridor. To meet this demand will require greater number and diversity in recreational facilities and improvements.

To alleviate some of the conflict between property owners and recreationalists will require additional public facilities and improvements within the parkway corridor. Some facilities and improvements can be developed at the time the parkway is constructed by taking advantage of opportunities along the route for pullouts, vista points and river access parkettes. Such amenities can be provided as part of the overall parkway development.

In addition, accessways, driveways, and roads to private property can be carefully located and designed to minimize conflict between the parkway visitor and local resident. Unsafe roadway conditions and potential traffic congestion must be minimized. The use and enjoyment of private property along the parkway is an important factor in managing the parkway corridor.

Issues of Parkway Alignment

The term, "parkway," is commonly associated with a parklike driving experience through scenic natural landscapes. These roadways are carefully designed to reveal to the driver the pleasurable qualities of the surrounding landscape. Many parkways in the country have provided such an enjoyable driving experience that they have become internationally recognized.

The New River Parkway is planned as a "touring parkway" passing through the diverse and dramatic landscapes of rural southern West Virginia. (The name for the New River Parkway was derived from a survey of local residents.) It will provide connection to Interstates 64 and 77 and serve as the principal gateway to the recreational resources and opportunities within the middle New River basin. The Parkway will provide direct access to the New River, Bluestone Lake, the Bluestone River, adjacent watershed slopes, stream valleys, and upper plateaus within the river basin. The Parkway, along its length, will also provide connection to other scenic rural roads which access adjacent areas of recreational, scenic, and historical value. These rural routes and spur roads form a network of scenic byways to serve both resident and visitor.

To accomplish this vision of a touring parkway system will require that the New River Parkway be designed by a recognized set of aesthetic principles of highway design.

The essential form of the touring Parkway should express its function, to move people safely and leisurely through the landscape. The Parkway should have a pleasing appearance, should fit gracefully into its surroundings, and become an integral part of the landscape. To accomplish this will require that the Parkway have minimum adverse impact on its environment, and provide pleasant visual experiences for the traveler.

The Parkway should be laid out to provide a variety of outward views of the country through which it passes. The location should take advantage of the finest views and vistas in the landscape.

The Parkway should appear to be in proper scale and fit the landscape without using excessive cuts and fills. Such fitting should be an important consideration when selecting the design speed and geometric standards for the road. An objective of the Parkway vision is to create a small scale, low speed touring road.

The Parkway should blend into the landscape as unobtrusively as possible with a minimum of scar and visual disruption. Unavoidable scars should be promptly healed or concealed by harmonious grading of landforms and appropriate planting to restore a natural appearance. The Parkway should allow the traveler an intimate experience of the adjacent landscape.

The Parkway should have a graceful three-dimensional appearance from the traveler's viewpoint. It should appear smooth, continuous, and predictable, without bumps or kinks. One of its aesthetic functions is to provide connection and continuity through diverse landscapes.

The Parkway right of way should be of sufficient width to accommodate the necessary facilities for present and future traffic; to provide adequate space for pullouts, vistas points, and parkettes; and to provide adequate space for stable rounded slopes, drainage channels, safe shoulders, and border transitions to adjacent areas. To the extent possible, parkway facilities and improvements should be located within the right of way.

Necessary structure and improvements, such as bridges, culverts, retaining walls, guardrails, and traffic control signs should be as unobtrusive as possible and should be of pleasing and appropriate design fitting the character and quality of adjacent landscapes.

Existing desirable vegetation within the right of way should be preserved to the greatest extent possible. The Parkway should be protected from erosion by living vegetation. Vegetation other than for erosion control such as trees and shrubs, should be selectively thinned or planted to maximize views and vistas and to help merge the roadsides into their surroundings.

Issues of Conserving Natural and Scenic Resources

The natural resources of the parkway corridor and its environs are an outstanding asset to West Virginia and to the nation as a whole. Many of these resources are the attraction that draws visitors to the region and the parkway corridor in particular. These natural resources need to be protected and managed to ensure that the opportunity to experience them will continue for future generations of residents and visitors alike.

These resources include the geology, soils, water quality, fisheries, wetlands, riparian habitats, wildlife, vegetation, air quality, and low level of noise.

Some of these resources are rare, threatened, and endangered species and unique habitats needing special protection and management. A portion of these resources are already protected and preserved in the New River Gorge National River and the Bluestone National Scenic River. The Parkway Authority intends to extend that protection to the entire parkway corridor.

The rocks along the parkway corridor are sedimentary formations that were deposited during the Mississippian and Pennsylvanian periods over 280 million years ago. The terrain within this region is essentially a deeply dissected plateau being cut by the river and its many tributaries. The resultant landforms tend to be rolling uplands, steep hill slopes and rugged gorges. Soils along the parkway corridor are mostly formed from shales and sandstones and tend to be shallow, rocky, of low fertility, but well suited for woodland and forest. Bottomlands along the river and gently sloping uplands provide the only opportunity for the cultivation of crops.

Water quality is generally good except for high levels of fecal coliform bacteria along certain reaches of the New River and its tributaries. In some cases, the levels of bacteria exceeds the West Virginia criterion for water contact recreation. High levels of fecal coliform bacteria indicates a lack of adequate sewage treatment for dwellings and communities along the river and in adjacent areas. In some cases raw sewage is leaching into the river or carried directly by tributary streams. Such a situation poses a health problem for recreationists and local communities alike.

The New River and its tributaries comprise the largest and most significant warm-water fishery in West Virginia and one of the best fisheries in the eastern United States. The New River supports and maintains game fish populations of a number of fish such as large mouth bass, catfish, and walleye. The river also has good spawning grounds in part provided by existing excellent habitat conditions. The maintenance and management of this vital resource is critical to ensure continued productivity. Issues of improving water quality, protecting productive habitat and backwater channels and islands are of major concern to the Parkway Authority.

The Parkway Authority, through application of the Land Management System, will ensure that all applicable state and federal regulations are followed in the protection and management of wetland resources along the parkway corridor.

Little is known about many of the wildlife populations of the New River and its tributaries. Rare, threatened, and endangered species are known to exist in the region, especially in riparian and aquatic habitats. Many of these species are listed on state and federal lists. Care should be exercised in planning, design, and location of public and private facilities and improvements along sensitive habitats. Wildlife could be threatened by poor water quality, the use of toxic chemicals, and the destruction of habitat from development.

The topographic diversity of the parkway corridor has led to the development of an unusual variation of flora, plant communities, and habitats. The landscape is characterized by the mixed mesophytic forests of deciduous trees and shrubs. Rare and endangered plant species occur within the parkway corridor at isolated sites, some in proximity to areas frequented by people and under use by utility companies. A relatively large flat rock plant community in Sandstone Falls supports rare and sensitive plant species. At least fifteen heritage sites have been identified within the immediate region. These sites have statewide ecological significance. Sensitive plant species and communities could be threatened by the use of toxic chemicals, construction, and trampling.

The Parkway Authority is concerned with the protection of these biological resources from unnecessary changes in plant communities and wildlife habitats especially adjacent to riverine systems. An important management strategy of the Parkway Authority will be to ensure minimum alteration of plant communities and vegetation to protect the natural hydrologic cycle.

Aesthetic resources are the most important key to the success of the New River Parkway. Outstanding features including views, vistas, natural land and water forms and historic and cultural features provide the scenic resource for the Parkway. The unique patterns of land use and topography give this region its own special character. While the appreciation of scenery is largely dependent upon the viewers own perception, the landscapes of this region are acknowledged by most people to be of outstanding character and quality.

How additional development might affect the visitor's appreciation of these scenic resources is of major concern to the Parkway Authority. The principle attraction of this region is found in the expression of a harmonious balance between human activity and the dynamics of nature and natural processes. It is therefore, critically important that all development, including the Parkway itself, be located, planned, and designed sensitively and with care to maintain the scenic integrity of the parkway corridor.

The Parkway Authority will implement the Parkway in a manner that minimizes the destruction and/or alteration of adjacent landscapes. Specifically, the parkway road and its related facilities and improvements will be designed, located, and constructed to minimize cut and fill sections, destruction or alteration of vegetative cover, ecotones and habitats, and loss or interruption of productive lands and land uses. Road improvements should not overwhelm or destroy the natural beauty of the parkway corridor. To integrate the Parkway into the landscape will require that the road be scaled to fit harmoniously into the landscape. If the quality of the touring experience is diminished by the character of roadway and roadside, then the quality of the overall recreational experience of the parkway corridor is, unfortunately, diminished.

To conserve, protect, and manage the scenic resource will require firm performance standards and design control over new developments. Site specific planning and design is necessary for each segment of the Parkway, for each structure, improvement or use. This is necessary to ensure that each new development or use fits into the overall scenic concept of the Parkway.

One of the best ways to ensure the overall visual integrity of the landscape in all its detail is to encourage visitor and resident stewardship of the parkway corridor's scenic beauty.

Issues of Conserving Cultural and Historical Resources

Cultural and historic resources in the parkway corridor and its environs are identified with the human use and settlement of the land. The New River was the primary corridor that linked the Ohio Valley to the ridges and valleys of the Appalachians and the Piedmont and coastal plain beyond. Indian trails and later trails of early migrants passed through this region. Roads and related developments were slow in coming to this rugged country. Turnpikes to scattered settlements followed waterways and natural passes through river gorges and upland plateaus. Early settlements served as remote centers for the hardy pioneers who sought a livelihood from the resources of the land. Major settlements occurred after the discovery of coal and timber resources and the construction of the Chesapeake and Ohio railroad lines into and through the region. Hinton grew as a railroad center serving many smaller settlements along the New River. Lumbering and agriculture supplemented the economy through the region as forests were cut and cleared to make way for fields and towns.

The remnants of forts, early roads, farms, and settlements still exist within the middle New River basin. The extent of these cultural resources is not known and their full historic significance is yet to be determined. Additional archaeological and historical research and study is needed to identify and evaluate these resources. It is the intent of the Parkway Authority to coordinate and cooperate with these researches whenever possible. The New River Parkway provides a unique opportunity to facilitate access to and interpretation of our cultural heritage.

It is the intent of the Authority to implement the Parkway in a manner that protects these cultural resources and minimizes the destruction and/or alteration of known sites and resources. The Authority will ensure that all applicable state and federal regulations are followed in the construction and development of parkway facilities and all new developments within the parkway corridor. The Authority will also encourage visitor and resident stewardship through the promotion and coordination of programs to preserve, restore and protect these resources.

Issues of Enhancing Recreational Opportunities

The opportunity for a wide range of outdoor recreation experiences is the principal attraction to much of this region. The region is rich in established recreation resources including the New River Gorge National River, Bluestone National Scenic River, Gauley River National Recreation Area, Pipestem State Park, Bluestone State Park, Camp Creek State Forest, and Bluestone Hunting and Fishing Area. The intent of the Parkway Authority is to tie together many of these outstanding recreational resources through the creation of the Parkway and a network of rural scenic byways.

Water-oriented recreation is a principle attraction of residents and visitors along the parkway corridor. Recreationists can participate in a range of active and passive activities from sight-seeing, picnicking, and hiking to fishing, swimming, and boating. Vacation resort facilities, such as those established at Pipestem State Park, provide a diverse balance to the more traditional outdoor recreation activities. Here within an hour's drive is a rich diversity of facilities and activity areas for all ages and interests. Collectively, the middle New River basin provides as full a complement of recreation activities as found in few areas in the country.

The intent of the Parkway Authority is to improve the accessibility to these outdoor recreation opportunities within the parkway corridor. At the present time, access to the recreational, scenic, and historical resources of the New River basin is restrained by an irregular network of secondary highways and substandard rural roads. These roads also serve as commercial arterials carrying truck traffic and daily commuters. The Parkway will provide a quiet, leisurely alternative to the busy interstates and highways which traverse portions of the basin.

Opportunities for accessibility also includes the provision of river access points for people and boats, access areas for day use and camping activities, tourist commercial facilities, adjacent communities, and nearby historical and cultural facilities.

To further complement the existing recreation resource potential, the Parkway Authority encourages new development that allows or provides use and enjoyment of the these resources. In addition to being an important link between established recreational facilities, the parkway corridor is a recreational resource in its own right. Recreational touring is the fastest growing outdoor recreation activity in the country. The parkway provides an outstanding opportunity for leisurely touring and sight-seeing through these scenic landscapes. Growth and change within the parkway corridor must be controlled and managed to ensure that the quality and character of this scenic landscape is preserved. Use and activities which do not serve the recreational intent of the Parkway should not be allowed as they detract from the overall recreational experience and, if allowed, would change the character and quality of the parkway corridor.

Goals and Objectives of the New River Parkway Authority

The New River Parkway Authority has adopted a set of goals and objectives to implement the Parkway and to guide the development of new land uses within the Parkway corridor. These goals and objectives evolved from a series of workshops and meetings with residents, civic groups, public officials, and Authority members. They provide the framework for policies to be formulated in the master plan which will implement provisions of the land management system.

Goal 1: Cooperative Venture

The New River Parkway will be implemented as a cooperative venture among private and public interests at all levels or organization.

OBJECTIVES:

- To facilitate the activities of nonvoting members regarding the New River Parkway.
- To establish comprehensive standards and guidelines for all new development within the Parkway corridor.
- To support and coordinate non-regulatory voluntary programs with interested individuals, agencies, and organizations.
- To support and coordinate educational programs with interested individuals, agencies, and organizations.
- To encourage the development of a visitor's facility to serve both the New River Parkway and the New River Gorge National River.

Goal 2: Economic Development

The New River Parkway will encourage economic development within the New River corridor.

OBJECTIVES:

- To support compatible economic development which benefits all West Virginia citizens.
- To support appropriate tourism development.

- To encourage land uses appropriate to the Parkway corridor.

Goal 3: Public Access

The New River Parkway will improve public access to the New River and other features while respecting private property rights.

OBJECTIVES:

- To provide safe and appropriate access to private property along the Parkway corridor.
- To provide safe and appropriate public access to the New River and its adjacent resources, including cultural, historical, natural, recreational, and scenic resources.

Goal 4: Parkway Alignment

The New River Parkway will be designed to fit sensitively and harmoniously into the diverse landscapes of the region.

OBJECTIVES:

- To create a small scale, low speed touring road.
- To provide connection and continuity through diverse landscapes.
- To implement the Parkway in a manner that allows an intimate experience of the adjacent landscape.
- To locate Parkway facilities and improvements within the Parkway right-of-way where possible.

Goal 5: Protect and Manage Natural Resources

The New River Parkway Authority will protect, manage, and interpret important natural resources of the Parkway corridor and its environs.

OBJECTIVES:

- To minimize alteration of vegetation to protect the hydrologic cycle.
- To restrict the introduction of sediments, nutrients, and toxic materials into the hydrologic cycle.
- To ensure that all applicable state and federal regulations are followed in the protection and management of wetland resources along the Parkway corridor.
- To minimize the destruction and degradation of habitats important to the use and enjoyment of the Parkway corridor.
- To ensure that all regulations are followed in cleaning up trash and litter along the Parkway corridor.
- To ensure that all regulations are followed in providing safe and adequate domestic water supplies and sanitation facilities.
- To ensure that all regulations are followed in conserving and protecting the low level of noise along the Parkway corridor from all sources.
- To ensure that all regulations are followed in protecting ambient air quality along the Parkway corridor from all sources.

Goal 6: Protect and Enhance Aesthetic Resources

The New River Parkway Authority will protect, manage, and enhance selected aesthetic resources of the Parkway corridor and its environs.

OBJECTIVES:

- To implement the Parkway in a manner that minimizes the destruction and/or alteration of adjacent landscape.
- To implement the Parkway in a manner that provides a scenic drive with a strong sense of visual continuity through diverse landscapes along the New River and on adjacent plateaus.
- To minimize the impact of urban infrastructure on the scenic quality of the Parkway corridor.
- To minimize the impact of new development on the scenic quality of the

parkway corridor.
- To encourage visitor and resident stewardship of the Parkway corridor's scenic beauty.

Goal 7: Protect Cultural and Historical Resources

The New River Parkway Authority will protect, manage, and interpret important cultural and historical resources of the New River corridor and its environs.

OBJECTIVES:
- To implement the Parkway in a manner that minimizes the destruction and/or alteration of cultural and historical resources.
- To ensure that all applicable state and federal regulations are followed in the protection and management of cultural and historical resources.
- To encourage visitor and resident stewardship of the Parkway's cultural and historical resources.

Goal 8: Enhance Recreation

The New River Parkway Authority will protect, manage, and enhance recreational resources important to the use and enjoyment of visitors and residents.

OBJECTIVES:
- To improve the accessibility of existing outdoor recreational resources of the region.
- To improve the accessibility to outdoor recreational experiences within the Parkway corridor.
- To encourage new development that allows recreational use and enjoyment of the New River and the Parkway corridor.

New River Parkway Concept Plan

The New River Parkway Concept Plan provides the vision for the creation of the Parkway and its corridor. It defines the overall goals and objectives for the Parkway and sets the conceptual framework for subsequent Master Plan and Land Management System.

The New River Parkway will be a touring parkway through the diverse and dramatic landscapes of southern West Virginia. It will provide the opportunity for a leisurely traveling experience offering views and vistas of rugged mountain slopes, river valleys, rural settlements, and scattered farms.

The Parkway will be designed to lie gracefully upon the land, becoming an integral part of the landscape as viewed from the road and to the road. It will be a small scale, low speed touring road offering a sequence of visual experiences in keeping with the character of its scenic corridor and beyond. The Parkway will offer the traveler an intimate experience of adjacent woods, streams, and fields.

The Parkway will provide essential linkages to Interstates 64 and 77 to facilitate safe and convenient access to the recreational and cultural resources of the middle New River basin. The Parkway will serve as the southern gateway to the New River Gorge National River and as the principle access to the Bluestone National Scenic River as well as other recreational and cultural facilities of regional and national importance.

The Parkway will provide touring facilities for the traveler along its length such as overlooks, safety pullouts, river access points, spur drives, parkettes, and trails. While the Parkway will be a destination facility in its own right, it will also provide connection to a network of scenic byways and rural roads to allow the traveler the opportunity to further explore the region.

The Parkway corridor, extending some 500 feet on either side of the road, will be protected under the provisions of the Parkway Authority's Land Management

System. Land use control will be established through corridor site plans, performance standards, and design guidelines for all new developments.

Appropriate land uses will be encouraged which are sensitively located and designed within the corridor and which support the goals and objectives of the Parkway. Tourist facilities will be encouraged which are in scale and harmony with the traditional rural character of the region, support the function of existing communities, and contribute to the quality of life of local residents. Land uses and activities incompatible with the policies of the Parkway Master Plan will be prohibited.

The Parkway provides the opportunity for interpretation of the cultural and natural landscape of the middle New River basin. This region, rich in history and scenic resources, offers visitors and residents alike the opportunity to experience the cultural landscape of the Appalachian Highlands. Interpretive programs and facilities will be established through the cooperative efforts of the Parkway Authority, public officials, civic organizations, and interested citizens.

The Parkway provides the opportunity to weave the richness and diversity of the natural, scenic, and cultural landscape of the middle New River basin into the fabric of reality and experience.

New River Parkway Master Plan

The New River Master Plan will guide the physical development of the Parkway and will protect and manage its scenic corridor. The Master Plan contains a set of comprehensive policies and diagrams that shows the existing and future alignment of the Parkway. The policies address the issues and concerns of residents, property owners, public officials, and Authority members. It serves as a firm guide for all new development, both public and private, within the scenic corridor.

The first function of the Master Plan is to express the goals, objectives, and policies of the New River Parkway Authority as established through numerous workshops, meetings, and studies, and as derived form the original concept plan and this document. Issues and concerns fundamental to the economic welfare and quality of life of residents within the middle New River basin were addressed through an open community participation process. The Master Plan reflects realistic goals for compatible uses and appropriate development over an extended period of time.

The second function is to serve as a guide to decision-making for local property owners and public officials. It indicates uses and activities appropriate for development within the parkway corridor, such as recreational uses and tourist facilities. It also limits uses not appropriate for inclusion, such as industrial and commercial enterprises not related to the recreational, cultural, and scenic experience of visitors to the parkway. The Master Plan reflects strong consensus and cooperation among local, state, and federal interests in the middle New River basin.

The Master Plan sets the scope and direction for the Land Management System which will implement land use policies.

New River Parkway Land Management System

The Land Management System contains the provisions necessary to implement adopted policies of the Master Plan within the parkway corridor. The Site Plan Review process is the procedure which will be used to implement the provisions and requirements of the Land Management System. This process will be activated through a permitting procedure by property owners or developers for new development within the Parkway corridor.

The system is composed of three interrelated elements: the scenic corridor site plan, design guidelines, and performance standards.

The scenic corridor site plan describes the opportunities and limitations for siting of structures, improvements, and activities along the corridor. This site plan controls the location of land uses relative to selected scenic resources of the Parkway as noted in the Master Plan.

Design guidelines illustrate how and what to do relative to site planning and design of structures, improvements, and activities within the scenic corridor. They provide a vision and example of appropriate site planning and design.

Performance standards specify levels of performance for uses and activities to conserve, protect, and management importance resources of the scenic corridor as specified in the Master Plan.

The Southern Appalachian Man and the Biosphere Cooperative

Hubert Hinote

I appreciate the opportunity to tell you about an organization that we believe will play an important role in resolving resource-related issues in our region. It's the Southern Appalachian Man and the Biosphere Cooperative, usually called SAMAB.

SAMAB's story begins with the great physical beauty of Southern Appalachia—a scenic magnet that has attracted visitors and new residents for many years.

This population growth has accelerated dramatically during the past two decades. So have demands on the natural resources of the mountains. Many resources have been depleted, some alarmingly.

The region today has problems with water supply and wastewater treatment, soil erosion and stream siltation, domestic and industrial waste disposal and air pollution, among others. These problems often are not dealt with adequately.

Without evidence to persuade them otherwise, many elected officials have upheld the traditional independence of Southern Appalachian people with regard to land use; *It's my land and I'll do as I damned well please with it,* has been perpetuated as an unwritten law.

The result is a scarcity of stewardship —in either a Biblical or a more modern sense. There are few land-use and zoning laws, and little in the way of growth-management strategies. There is inadequate resource-protection regulation by government.

This has resulted in philosophical clashes between individuals and groups who take extreme stands on many resource-related issues. One side usually wants relatively unrestricted use of natural resources. The other side has seen the results of uncontrolled growth and development elsewhere and tends to advocate total preservation.

Neither position is completely right, nor completely wrong. Although there has been negative use of natural resources over the years, use of those resources has had a positive effect on the economy and the well-being of people of the region.

The problem is that extremists' arguments often are founded more on emotion than on facts. Meanwhile, it has been difficult to bring facts into the equation.

That's because there isn't enough documented natural resource and economic data to (1) convince either side of an issue that opposing arguments might have validity, and (2) to provide a realistic basis for remedial policy or legislation.

What's badly needed is solid scientific information that can help dissolve much of the disunity, and, at the same time, provide a basis for sensitive decision making by public resource managers, private developers and elected officials.

Reacting to this situation, a number of Federal agencies with regional interests got together in the mid-1980s to explore the concept of an organization that could become a source for this much-needed data.

It quickly became apparent that in order for such an organization to be successful, it would have to:

1. Recognize the need for economic development *and* resource conservation in the Southern Appalachian region;

2. Have the capability to generate economic and natural resource data

germane to specific regional issues;
3. Become recognized as a voice of reason by moderates *and* extremists;
4. Become a source of information for elected officials responsible for legislation to protect and enhance the interests of all parties.

These stipulations eventually became the operational guidelines for the Southern Appalachian Man and the Biosphere Cooperative.

Officials representing six Federal agencies and bureaus agreed in August 1988 to work jointly and provide initial financial support for SAMAB. Charter members were the:

Economic Development Administration, National Park Service, Oak Ridge National Laboratory, Tennessee Valley Authority, U.S. Fish & Wildlife Service and U.S. Forest Service.

Since, the Environmental Protection Agency and the U.S. Geological Survey have become members of the Cooperative. The Appalachian Regional Commission, U.S. Army Corps of Engineers and Soil Conservation Service are considering membership.

In addition, the State of Georgia has joined, while Alabama, North Carolina, South Carolina, Tennessee and Virginia, all of which have lands within the SAMAB zone of cooperation, have been invited to also become active state partners.

The *Zone of Cooperation* I mentioned is a somewhat loosely defined mountainous area that includes five designated units of the Southern Appalachian Biosphere Reserve—the Great Smoky Mountains National Park, Coweeta Hydrologic Laboratory in the Nantahala National Forest, the National Environmental Research Park at Oak Ridge, Tennessee, Grandfather Mountain, and Mt. Mitchell State Park.

There are more than 260 Biosphere Reserves throughout the world. All have been designated by the United Nations Educational, Scientific and Cultural Organization (UNESCO) as areas worthy of preservation because of their unique natural resources or usefulness in studying human impacts on the land.

Designation of an area as a Biosphere Reserve does not, and I emphasize not, bring with it any regulatory authority; there are no restrictions on private land use within or adjacent to it. It is not a covert means of expanding the public land base. It does not give *Big Brother* another way to dictate what can or cannot be done on the land. In other words, as a television comedian once said, "What you see is what you get."

Within this framework, and with its extensive and diverse membership, SAMAB easily has the expertise to thoroughly comply with its mission statement, which is:

> To foster harmonious relationships between humans and their environment through programs and projects that integrate the social, physical and biological sciences to address actual problems.

I wish I could tell you that SAMAB already has been smashingly successful in meeting all of its challenges. I regret that I cannot—yet.

I can say, however, that some impressive first steps have been taken.

Actively addressing some of the situations and problems affecting people and their environment in the Southern highlands, SAMAB has provided leadership for a number of actions, including:

A model program at Pittman Center, Tennessee, to demonstrate that tourism and natural resource protection can be compatible.

Free informational meetings to inform the public of threats posed by a fungal disease (dogwood anthracnose) to the native flowering dogwood tree.

Environmental education programs for Grades K-8 on the Great Smoky Mountains National Park Biosphere Reserve and the Southern Appalachian Region.

Production of the first of what will be annual conferences to address prominent environmental issues in the region.

Creation of a tax-exempt, nonprofit foundation that provides an avenue for private sector, university and other involvement in SAMAB.

Preparation of informational literature and close contact with regional media to make SAMAB's presence, role and mission more well known.

Thus, after a relative brief existence, SAMAB appears to be on its way toward earning a permanent and respected niche in environmental and economic affairs in Southern Appalachia.

The diversity of its membership gives SAMAB the ability to examine issues and problems from a *big picture* perspective. This helps eliminate any agency bias and ensures that the Cooperative is recognized as a voice of sound judgment.

I don't have a crystal ball that will allow me to look into SAMAB's future, but one doesn't have to be a fortune teller to see some things clearly.

First and foremost, SAMAB's responses to environmental and economic questions and issues will continue to be based on a broad spectrum of knowledge and delivered without the stamp of any particular area of interest.

However, in order to achieve long-term success, SAMAB first must solidify some important short-term goals. These include:

1. Continued support by members until financial independence is achieved through support by the SAMAB Foundation.

2. Sound cooperative working relationships with universities and organizations involved in natural and cultural resource, social and economic research.

3. An agency compatible, computerized database (geographic information system, or GIS) on the ecosystems of the Southern Appalachian region.

4. Leadership for other regional groups that are considering or following SAMAB'S example.

In conclusion, the need for an organization such as SAMAB in the Southern Appalachians is evident, as it is in many other areas where the forces of use and preservation are in competition.

While SAMAB has made significant positive strides in a relatively short time, many steps remain to be taken.

If these steps are taken successfully, the natural and cultural resources of Southern Appalachia will be better protected, visitors will be able to see and enjoy them, and residents of the region will prosper economically.

www.ingramcontent.com/pod-product-compliance
Lightning Source LLC
Chambersburg PA
CBHW031150160426
43193CB00008B/320